FRESH OUT OF THE BAPTISMAL POOL

A Guide for New Christians Ensuring Growth in Jesus Christ

Brandon Dusanic

Copyright © 2024 Brandon Dusanic
All rights reserved.

*This book is dedicated to Liam and Kellyn.
Thank you for believing in me.
Love Dad*

TABLE OF CONTENTS

Introduction		vii
Chapter 1	Congratulations and Welcome to the Family!	1
Chapter 2	The Enemy	11
Chapter 3	Church	26
Chapter 4	The Bible	37
Chapter 5	Small Groups	49
Chapter 6	Mentorship	61
Chapter 7	Service and Volunteerism	72
Chapter 8	Leadership	82
Chapter 9	Evangelism	93
Chapter 10	Reflection and Prayer	105
Conclusion		119
About the Author		129

INTRODUCTION

Be watchful, stand firm in the faith, act like men, be strong. Let all that you do be done in love.

—1 Corinthians 16:13–14

Thank you for picking up a copy of my book. You are probably asking yourself the who, what, where, when, why, and how questions about what is on the pages. I am just a regular guy who loves Jesus and his family. Armed with a degree in biblical studies, I wanted to understand the past fifteen years since I became a follower of Christ and how God has been with me through some awful valleys and inspiring mountains. I began to reflect on my life and realized the many pitfalls and missteps I took in the infancy of my walk with Christ. I also saw the solutions to my problems. This book is the result of my journey and is intended to outline suggestions and helpful hints that will assist new believers in their walks with Christ and ensure growth.

Other books are available on this subject, which have been written by world-renowned pastors and teachers of the Word of God. I highly encourage you to check them out. The more knowledge you can gain, the better. But what makes this book different? What makes this book different is that it is written NOT from the perspective of a theologian or pastor; it is written by someone who walked the road that you, the new Christ follower, are walking down right now! This book is not just theoretical; it has practical application to your early walk with Christ. This book is written by a regular and flawed person who has experienced the struggles of "getting in where you fit in" within the local church. A person who sometimes struggles to understand the Bible and its meaning. A person who had to battle real-world daily struggles without the knowledge crutch of a seminary degree. I am just like you! I stumbled through the first decade of my walk with Christ, and I do not want you to do the same.

After reflecting on my own life, I learned that God needed me to walk through all the exciting and mind-boggling times to write this book and inspire others not to make the same mistakes as a young Christian. I feel called to write this book. I feel called to spend a couple of hours a day in front of a laptop typing away to improve one person's life. I do not have a book deal with a publisher. I have an open Word document, an open Bible, and an open heart to hear God. I pray that this book is a well-written and practical outline for you, the new follower of Christ, so you can experience growth and immediately impact the kingdom of God.

My religious background is probably pretty much like yours as well. I did not grow up in the church. I remember growing up and occasionally attending my grandparents' red brick Southern Baptist church in rural Virginia on a random Sunday. Church was so uncomfortable. It was hot, and the sounds of old men grunting "amen" after everything being said permeated the air. Random people dressed in their Sunday best would shake my hand and tell me how I grew up like a weed. We would take our seats in the long, wooden pews. The pews had a fabric covering them that I still have not felt anywhere else other than those pews. A short, chubby man would lead the choir out, and suddenly, an organ would start playing, and the congregation would half-heartedly start singing a hymnal. Then an older gentleman with silver hair stepped up to the pulpit and proceeded to scare the poop out of me. For the next hour and a half of my life, I learned precisely why and how I was to be tormented in Hell because of my thoughts and actions. It was a frightening experience. My grandmother was my refuge because she would have Lifesaver Wintergreen mints or Tic Tacs in her purse, and she would sneak me through the service. It seemed like an eternity while I listened to the message. My anxiety levels would rise and fall with the ebb and flow of the voice of the pastor. Then, as fast as it began, it would be over. People would get up and walk past the pastor and tell him that he gave an excellent sermon. Meanwhile, I had no idea what he was talking about the whole time. I just knew that I was a naturally inadequate person and that to stay out of Hell, I needed to follow a former carpenter named Jesus Christ. This was my introduction to Christianity. Doesn't that sound appealing?

> <u>Halftime Scripture</u>: *Therefore, if anyone is in Christ, the new creation has come: The old has gone, the new is here!*
>
> *—2 Corinthians 5:17*

I did not attend church from when I was ten until adulthood. I was petrified of it. Plus, I enjoyed sleeping in on Sundays. I also enjoyed fishing and other shenanigans. My grandparents would still invite me to church, but I had my own life to live. High school and college came, and I believed just about whatever the hottest women believed in. That was my idol as a young man. Women.

Fresh out of the Baptismal Pool

God knew this, though, and that is when he sent my now ex-wife into my life. She was the most beautiful woman I had ever seen, and she wanted to talk to me for some reason. During our brief courtship, she asked me if I was a follower of Christ and if I would go to church with her. If she had asked if I were a Buddhist, I would have shaved my head and donned one of those neat robes. Luckily, she was a Christian and reintroduced me to the church. God has a fantastic way of setting up the building blocks of a person's life. Looking back, it is nothing short of miraculous what he did.

Fast-forward a bit, and I became a married husband and father. My wife wanted to ensure that our kids were raised in a "Christian" household with "Christian" values at the center of everything we did. At the time, I subscribed to the Happy Wife, Happy Life way of thinking. We began to attend a church in sunny San Diego. Like most things in California, it was a completely different church experience than I had in rural Virginia. Men were wearing shorts! Fancy coffee was being served outside the sanctuary. There were no hymnals to memorize, and the words were plastered on screens everywhere. There were hot tubs outside for some reason; I did not understand that until later. The church reminded me of a cross between an airport, mall, and office complex. It was completely different from what I had grown up with. People were friendly and close to my age. No old men in suits were grunting "amen" at random times during the sermon. To this day, I still do not understand why those old fellas would randomly holler during church. Especially when the pastor was not even talking. Maybe when I turn sixty-five and qualify for social security, I will start doing that, too.

The message the pastor preached seemed different, too. I was not scared during the sermons. I don't think Hell, fire, and brimstone were mentioned in the two years we attended church there. I learned about love, sacrifice, and integrity while I was there. I began reading the Bible and studying it for the first time. I tried desperately to understand the Bible. I started believing in Christ finally. I felt understood, protected, and a part of something bigger than myself. After about two years, I decided to take the plunge and become a full-fledged follower of Christ. I asked Jesus to come into my heart and save me. He did, and I was saved! After accepting Christ as my Lord and Savior, I signed up to get baptized in those hot tubs I thought were so cool when I first started attending church. My wife and I both got baptized on the same chilly November evening. It was excellent, and even though my wife and I are no longer together, I am still thankful as she was the igniting force behind my love and acceptance of Christ.

According to the pastor and what I understood of the Bible, the game of life had been won! I was not going to go to Hell. I was going to live forever with my Savior. The blood of Jesus saved me! I had successfully filled out the forms and requirements for fire insurance. However, being a Christ follower is so much more. I became a Christian initially for selfish reasons, but God uses everything for the good of his plan. I did not realize what I had signed up for.

Little did I know the daily battles a follower of Christ will face. To say I was ill-equipped to fight in those battles would be an understatement. I later learned that many things that make sense to us here on Earth have no relative bearing in Heaven. Yes, Jesus won the war over death, Hell, and the grave. He won the war over Satan and all things in this world. However, daily individual battles still needed to be fought. In my mind, battles are fought so that a war can be won. But Christ won the war before any struggle could ever be fought. Confusing. How could a war have been won two thousand years ago, yet daily battles still exist? Something was not adding up. I had so much learning to do, and it was wild!

Churches and pastors in the local church do a fantastic job of getting people to accept Christ and be saved, but when it comes to practical steps after the immersion, we, as a church, could do much better. In my own experience, I was left alone to figure it all out. In a hot tub in San Diego, I thought I had won life. I had no idea that I needed to put on the armor of God every day. In my opinion, we in the Western church are set up not to fail because Christ will not allow us to fail but to endure needless suffering. After all, we are not equipped for what comes after being baptized. I know because I went through it, and after years of counseling, honest meditation, and reflection, I can see what I did wrong. The traps that were being set for me to walk in. The feelings of loneliness, guilt, and pleasure-seeking that are made to destroy people. Looking back on my life, I can see how the enemy placed all these things to trip me up and minimize my impact on the world. If you are a human being, know that you are in a daily battle with Satan.

In my fifteen years of being a follower of Christ, I have been put through the wringer. Health scares, career changes, depression, anxiety, grief, and every painful situation and emotion you can think of I have walked through. I felt so inadequate at times. Sometimes, I felt like I was being punished for something I did in the past. When I would seek Godly counsel, I was met with people who I knew had to be going through things like what I went through but who had donned a mask to prevent others from knowing. I would attend Bible studies and felt like the prayer request time was a joke. Why was I having all these deep problems and issues, and why was no one else having them? I would question my salvation constantly! It was not until one day, during a Bible study, that I called out my other Bible study patrons and laid out everything that was keeping me up at night. I emotionally vomited on a golf course clubhouse patio furniture table in front of a handful of men I barely knew. Afterward, it was silent. Those poor fellas did not know what to say. They had been focused on the superficial skin-deep issues but not the deep ones. Luckily, God was not finished. It was only the beginning. Looking back, I realize that more growth happened to me after that day than ever before. True Christianity gets filthy, dirty fast. It is not all praises and happy days like it is sometimes depicted in our society today. It can be gut-wrenching. It is needed, though. Our world needs truthful and profound Christianity. We need Christ more now than ever! I spent fifteen years banging my head against the wall and getting in my very own way.

I had no guidance after I was saved and baptized. This book is intended to be a roadmap for you to detour around all the mess the enemy puts in front of you and keep your eyes on Jesus. In the Bible, Ephesians 6:11 talks about putting on the armor of God, and believe me, you will need every bit of armor to withstand the daily onslaught that Satan throws at you. Each chapter of my book has an opening scripture for you to read and meditate on. It also has a "Halftime Scripture" to read and meditate on halfway through each chapter. At the end of the chapters are "keep it simple steps," a proverb to read, and a verse about baptism to look up and write on the blank line on the next page if you want to. My goal is for you to get the most out of this book.

Christianity is not a Sunday morning where you dress up, converse with friends, attend a concert, listen to a motivational speaker, and then attend a fish fry fundraiser. Christianity is a war against unimaginable powers. After becoming a follower of Jesus, I unknowingly enlisted in his army and was instantly put in the crosshairs of Satan. I had no idea at the time what I would go through over the next several years in my walk with Christ. I would become a battle-tested warrior with a privileged and weak latte-inspired faith. My prayer is that you do not go through what I went through. Understand that Satan is deceptive and will try to trip you up. Often, he will succeed in doing so. He will use everything in his arsenal to minimize your impact on God's kingdom. Satan does not want you to bring more people into the arms of Jesus. He wants to shame you and use your past, flaws, and weaknesses to impact others' viewpoints on Christ. This book is meant to help you as a new believer in navigating life after accepting Christ and being baptized. Your salvation in Christ is not the end of the race. It is just the beginning! Looking back at my life, this book lists things I should have done to give me a more stable situation in which to grow as a Christian. You cannot succeed in Christ without other people and joyful work!

Keep It Simple Step: If you just got baptized, take a moment to celebrate that accomplishment! Throw a party with friends or relatives. Go to a nice dinner. Do whatever you like to celebrate this event! People are

Fresh out of the Baptismal Pool

constantly partying about things that do not matter, like sporting events or concerts. Your decision to follow Jesus Christ is a billion times more important than whoever wins a Super Bowl or Championship game. Celebrate *You* and *Your* decision in some way! This is the most crucial decision you have ever made, and you deserve to be joyful and celebrate it!

Where there is no revelation, the people cast off restraint, but happy is he who keeps the law.

—Proverbs 29:18

<u>Read and journal on Genesis Chapters 7 and 8.</u>

CHAPTER 1
CONGRATULATIONS AND WELCOME TO THE FAMILY!

> *Therefore, if anyone is in Christ, the new creation has come: The old has gone, the new is here!*
>
> —*2 Corinthians 5:17*

If you are reading this book, you are probably thinking about becoming a follower of Christ or have already become a follower of Christ. Let me start by telling you that if you are a new follower of Christ, welcome to the family! New members must make the coffee in the morning and take out the trash at night. Just kidding. I wish it were that easy. Seriously, though, welcome to the family. To those who are thinking about following Christ, please do it! You can make no better decisions in your life and your family's life. Your decision will span multiple generations and influence those you love and are close to, as well as your community at large. Christ does not call us to do much. He calls us to do what matters most! God initially gave us the Ten Commandments, but we could not get that right. Christ wants us to love him and our neighbor when we get down to the nitty-gritty of the gospel. If you are thinking about becoming a follower of Christ, do not listen to the naysayers or faithless people on TikTok and Instagram. There is a reason why you are drawn to Christ and curious about the faith. Find a local church and ask questions! Pastors love getting asked questions. Especially the deep ones. It inspires them to study more and makes them better pastors. If the pastor you find does not take time to answer your questions, find another one. Remember that pastors are human, and humans are imperfect. Do not get discouraged.

I do not know where you are in your journey, but I want you to understand that you are on a mission for Jesus Christ once you become saved. What is your mission, you ask? That is found through studying the Bible, prayer, meditation, and utilizing God-given gifts that support your calling or purpose to further the kingdom of God. Not this book. I am still figuring it out. I am not equipped to enlighten you on the secrets of life. Sorry! I want you to realize the enormous undertaking you took on when you were saved.

Hopefully, your church had you take a class or Bible study that walked you through what it meant to be a Christian and to be saved before you took the plunge and got saved and baptized. Not all churches do this, but some do. Maybe your church even partnered you up with a mentor or someone to ask questions that arise. Maybe someone prayed with you and for you. If that is the case, you are ahead of the game. Consider yourself lucky to have a church with those programs. Following Christ is a personal decision, but it is not intended to be an individual and personal journey. It would be best if you had people. Good people. Not perfect people but good, Christ-centered people.

In my experience, local churches do an excellent job of reaching out and going about the business of saving people's lives. They do a great job of loving a community of believers and going about the "Great Commission" Christ gave us. If you need to know the "Great Commission," look it up! In a nutshell, it tells believers of Christ to go out and make new disciples. The churches may even have trackers that track the number of people saved and baptized for a given year. That is fantastic and gives a tangible number to the growth of God's kingdom in a specific area or community. However, what does a person do after being "dunked" in the water? After the celebration. After the party, the fish fry is complete, and the cake is gone. What happens next? Looking back on my life, I now realize that what happens is a daily battle. Christ meant it when he said, "Take up your cross and follow me." Daily spiritual hand-to-hand combat, not over your soul, because that is already won, but against the powers of darkness in this world who see you as the enemy. Powers of darkness that cannot do anything to you but want to discourage others from following your path to freedom in Christ. Powers of darkness that are trying to knock you down so that others see fault in not only you but your battlefield commander, Jesus Christ.

Before you get too scared and run off, understand that Christ will equip you for the battles. However, churches do not usually have the time on Sunday morning to tell you practically how to unlock and utilize the equipment needed for battle. Your battlefield commander is right beside you. Everything you need has already been given to you. But you are a fresh soldier for Christ who has not yet gotten off the bus for basic training. Before a soldier, sailor, or marine can become a lethal weapon for the country, they must go through basic training. Reflecting on my life, I can see that I missed the bus for basic training in spiritual warfare. Do not be me. The local church is the recruit training center for Christ. Utilize everything they offer after being saved. If the sanctuary doors are open, be there with bells on. Join a Bible study. Volunteer. Find a mentor. Find a 2:00 a.m.

friend. Pray. Be vulnerable in the house of God, with the people of God, so they can honestly know and help you. Church is a lot of things, and military-style base is one of them. Use it and train! Train like you have never trained before in your life. Following Christ is not a full-time job or hobby. It is a real-life war zone that you are walking into, and it needs to be treated as such.

One extensive criticism of the Western church in America is that we must step away from the coffee bar and focus on rediscovering who our enemy is and preparing our church members for the daily battles they will incur. A "Christ-Light Social Club" will not get the job done. It is only going to create weak soldiers for Christ, especially with the constant bombardment of misinformation on social media. Those subliminal videos spreading false truths are done by none other than Satan himself. We must develop church members who can see through the poppycock and withstand the bombardment that the devil throws at us. The kingdom of Heaven needs strength, courage, and steadfast leadership that mirrors its commander-in-chief, Jesus. But how do we get it? We get it through intentional training and mentorship of church members.

> <u>Halftime Scripture</u>: *And let us consider how we may spur one another on toward love and good deeds, not giving up meeting together, as some are in the habit of*

> *doing, but encouraging one another—and all the more as you see the Day approaching.*
>
> *—Hebrews 10:24–25*

But how do you know you are in the right church? There are currently over 350,000 Christian churches in the United States, which means you have plenty of options. To put this in perspective, there are only 13,000 McDonald's restaurants in the country. There is a buffet smorgasbord of churches for the new Christ follower to go to and find a home in. How do you know you are in the right one? Do not overthink it. Ask yourself a few simple questions.

The first question to ask yourself is, do I feel comfortable here? If we are all being honest, we feel most comfortable around people who are like us. It is okay to ask yourself this non-politically correct question. For example, if you are a young, single mother, do you think that your grandmother's church, without a nursery and everyone being an octogenarian, is going to be the best place for you to grow in Christ? It might be, but I doubt it. That young, single mom would probably be better suited to a church with a younger congregation with a children's ministry. Be completely honest. Celebrities are wrong when saying, "Only God can judge me." If you walk into a church on a Sunday with a group of people unlike you, everyone is judging. I do not think they mean to. It is just human nature. So, find a church that you are comfortable in.

The next question would involve some research. Over 200 denominations of Christianity are currently operating in the United States, while over 45,000 are worldwide. This is a staggering number to me since only one Jesus Christ exists. Make sure the denomination of the Christian church aligns with your values. Some do not, and that is okay. You may not want to be a snake handler in the rural denomination of the Church of God with Signs Following. Maybe you do! It is up to you! Take a moment and do some research on the church you are attending. Ask a pastor what is different about this church than the other 199.

The final question to ask about the church you are attending is how much time is spent reading the Bible. Remember that church is not a political rally or a motivational secret of a success seminar at the airport Holiday Inn. Church is many things, but it is not either of those. Ask yourself, is the Bible being taught during the sermons? Do not become captivated by the pastor unless he speaks from and about the Word of God! Several trendy churches in the United States will go through entire sermons and not reference one scripture. How do I know this? Watch the televangelists on television at 3:00 a.m. They might not have the best intentions if they attempt to sell you "holy water" or a "prayer shawl" more than they reference the Bible.

Your local church should be your second home. You should be able to be your true self with people. You should be able to grow. To feel like a sponge and soak up all the knowledge you can about Jesus. Church should be where you feel like you *get* to go and do not *have* to go. Make your local church your home base for your ministry for Christ! You may not believe it now, but Christ is preparing you for ministry.

This book is intended to be a guide. To show practical and meaningful steps not always easily advertised or known by new Christ followers to grow your faith. I was baptized and turned loose into the world. This is not an intelligent way of doing things. Think of a baby being born. That baby, after birth, is at its most vulnerable directly out of the womb. It takes an entire team to huddle around, nurture, and be there to watch it grow. This book will show the new believer the actions and places within the church to seek that safety net so that they do not get shot down after being born again in Christ. This book is intended for the new Christ followers right after they dry off from the baptism. I wish everyone peace and growth in Christ. Go forward, fight on, and change the world for the better, one person at a time.

Keep It Simple Step: Participate actively in a local church community, attending services, joining small groups or Bible studies, and contributing your talents to serve others within the church. Start small; maybe shoot for two Sunday services in a row. Next thing you know, you are a regular attender.

The fear of the LORD is the beginning of knowledge, but fools despise wisdom and instruction.

—Proverbs 1:7

Brandon Dusanic

<u>Read and journal on Exodus chapter 14.</u>

CHAPTER 2
THE ENEMY

*Be sober, be vigilant; because your adversary
the devil, as a roaring lion, walketh about,
seeking whom he may devour.*

—*1 Peter 5:8*

Intelligence is the key to winning any war. Knowing everything about your enemy is how you find and exploit a weakness for victory. Satan is real. He is not a made-up fictional character. He is everything and more than you can imagine. He is the bully on the block who steals your lunch money and then scr*ws your mind so badly that you feel sorry for him. He is the prince of darkness. He is the serpent. He is the bad guy. He is alive and is the enemy we are up against daily. He is our enemy and keeps us in chains of sin.

Right after Jesus Christ was baptized, he went to the wilderness to be tested, and for lack of a better term, he battled Satan for forty days. Now, that happened to the Son of God. Satan is so full of himself that he tries to trip up the Son of God! He tried to discourage and tempt the Son of God! Let that sink in for a minute. If you do not, for a second, think that Satan is not going to try to discourage you and ruin your life after you commit and are saved by Jesus Christ, you are living in a fairy-tale land. Satan has always been after you. I hate saying it, but up until Christ saved you, you were on Satan's team. To take an analogy from sports, you were in a contract with team Satan, became a free agent, and signed with team Jesus. Team Satan and his fans now hate you! It's like you played for the Philadelphia Eagles and then signed with the Dallas Cowboys. Except multiplied by infinity, the amount of hatred that Satan now has for you. He will go after you with everything he has at his disposal.

I felt the crosshairs of Satan landing on me quickly after I became a believer. Depression and addiction have always run deep in my family, and I was not spared those genes. It was a textbook situation for a deep, depressive episode that was meant to derail my life. I was in a career field I could not get out of. My kids were having all kinds of issues. My marriage was filled with doubt and contempt. I was always sad and angry. It seemed like my life was spiraling out of control. I could not take it anymore. Eventually, I ended up broken after the pills could not control the horrible feelings I battled. I pleaded with God to take the pain away. Looking back at that time, I now realize what Satan was doing. He knew he could not win my soul back. But what he did was he undermined me and prohibited me from spreading the gospel.

People at work would ask me why I acted differently, etcetera, and I would boldly exclaim, "I am a Christian! That is why I am different." But once people saw my life in shambles or me not toeing the line as a Christ follower, they had doubts that what Christ offered was not all it was cracked up to be. That they were perfectly fine where they were at. They thought everything I believed was a lie because my life was in shambles or I had stumbled and sinned. Satan used me and my weaknesses as a human being to dissuade those around me from accepting Christ as their savior! Satan was and is still playing chess while I play checkers in the game of life. He is a deceiver and master manipulator. The Bible shows believers that Jesus won the war. Satan is merely trying to scr*w over as many people as he can before the end-times.

Understand that this complete breakdown that I had did not happen overnight. It was a culmination of little things that accumulated over time. Like a leaky bathroom faucet, it was a drip-drip method to break me down and minimize my evangelical impact. It was a slip-of-the-tongue curse word here. An extended glance at an attractive woman there. A tiny fib to get out of work early here. An embellishment on an evaluation or award there. All these sins added up to cause doubt in those around me whom I was supposed to be reaching, and I did not even see it! I continued to be a regular human being. Satan is so clever at deceiving us. He has made our society so far removed from righteousness that even good-hearted Christians do not realize when they are sinning anymore. He knows that he cannot get to the saved. So, he goes about his work, bringing doubts to those around him.

Sadly, our own Westernized "prosperity gospel" focuses on the material blessings that we, as Christians, should receive in response to our faith. Which is never actually said anywhere in the Bible. Look for it in the Bible! I promise, nowhere in the good book does it say that you will receive blessings if you give the church money. Even church leadership can often be blinded by Satan. How many times have you ever been driving by a massive church with multiple fancy cars in the staff parking lot and thought that does not seem right? Sarcastically thinking, those pastors sure are giving all the money to the poor, aren't they? It's because it isn't! The fact that you had those thoughts when looking at a house of God is precisely the undermining that Satan wants to do! Money is never going to fix problems. Joyful work, supportive relationships, and prayer will.

But Satan knows that money reigns supreme in this world we live in. If we are honest, money is our idol. We would do anything for more money, and Satan sees this weakness. I am sure he created money or drives our lust for it. How do we battle it? With knowledge, of course! What does the Bible say about money? Not what Satan is saying or making our society think about it. Heck, Jesus said to sell all your belongings and follow him. So, that is where Christ stands on the idea of money.

When nonbelievers see believers struggling daily, it casts doubt on them. I mean, look at our American society. Churches are on every street corner, and still, poverty and plight are everywhere among members of our church. We are hurtful and imperfect people. Satan knows that and is using it to chip away at people we encounter daily. He cannot get to believers anymore. We broke free from his bondage. So, he uses us as imperfect people to tighten the chains on those who have not yet believed. Our job as Christians is not to be perfect people—it is impossible—but to lead by example and bring others in our community closer to Christ. We cannot do this on our own. It takes so many practical steps that I often feel like we, as a church, overlook as new members of the faith join the ranks. Satan realizes this weakness, and it is where he attacks us first.

But what is a practical way for a new Christ follower to stand up and fight against Satan? Amazingly, it is found in the Bible. The Bible is going to be the place where the warriors for Christ make our stands. It will take time, and it will be difficult because of sin. Recall that the Bible says that the demons will tremble and flee at the mention of the name of Jesus!

The most practical beginning steps to battle Satan found in the Bible are in Ephesians chapters 4 to 6. This is not the only place, but it is a good outline of how believers in Christ are to act in a world that is bombarded by sin and the traps laid out by Satan. Ephesians chapters 4 to 6 touch on all kinds of subject matter, primarily how to act in the many roles we take on in our daily lives. Daily items like speaking foolishly about how we treat our spouses and children. Do not overthink it! Just be open to the information found in the pages of the Bible. Ephesians 6 ends with the famous explanation of people putting on the whole armor of God. So, all believers, girdle your loins and don the entire armor of God. Prepare to battle Satan daily and help those around us find salvation with Christ Jesus.

This book is about practicality, so what does it look like in 2024 to don the whole armor of God? To prepare oneself for battle daily against the evil in this world. James 4:7 says, "Resist the Devil, and he will flee from you." But what does that mean? Let's break it down simply together. In Ephesians Chapter 6:10–17, the apostle

Paul uses the metaphor of spiritual armor to illustrate the concept of preparing to do spiritual warfare. Each practical piece of armor has meaning attached to it and will help you withstand the daily onslaught thrown at you by the enemy.

The first piece is the "Belt of Truth." Truth is foundational to how we live out our lives as followers of Christ. It represents living a life based on God's truth and being honest and upright in all dealings. Essentially, it tells the new believer in Christ to be truthful and have integrity in everything they do. How does a regular everyday person don the belt of truth? The best way to don the belt of truth is to start your day with God's word, the Bible. Read scripture at the start of every day and place God's truth in your heart and mind. That way when confronted with issues that may seem counter to your walk with Christ, you can compare the truth of God's word to that issue.

Next is the "Breastplate of Righteousness." This piece protects the heart. It signifies living a life of moral integrity and righteousness, which guards against Satan's attacks. It is funny, but the best way to arm yourself with this spiritual armor is to surrender to God and his standards. Practically, for the new believer, this means to put God first and pray. Prayer is an essential practice for a follower of Christ. An entire chapter is devoted to this. Prayer is going to remind you to seek God and put him first. To remind your heart who is protecting you and on your side. Usually, all you need is a moment of praise and prayer, and clarity is found for whatever you are dealing with!

> <u>Halftime Scripture:</u> *And the devil, who deceived them, was thrown into the lake of burning sulfur, where the beast and the false prophet had been thrown. They will be tormented day and night forever and ever.*
>
> *—Revelation 20:10*

Additionally, are the "Shoes of the Gospel of Peace." These shoes represent readiness and preparedness to share the gospel of peace with others. They enable believers to stand firm and move swiftly in spreading the message of Christ. This armor might be the scariest for you as a new believer. To spread the gospel to others and be ready to stand up for Christ in all situations. It is nerve-racking to think that we could potentially lose a job or a friend for our belief in Christ, but it is a genuine possibility. Christ talks about this in the Bible. So, how does a new believer share the gospel? A new believer can best share the gospel by obeying God's word. Actions speak louder than words. People will notice that you have changed since being saved. When they ask you questions, you can respond with Jesus, which is why X, Y, and Z happened. Once you have grown more in the faith, you should feel more comfortable sharing the gospel with anyone and everyone!

Following that is the "Shield of Faith." The shield is used to extinguish the flaming arrows of the evil one. Faith in God's promises and protection shields against doubts, fears, and temptations. This is a hard one to combat practically because it takes faith in Jesus Christ to constantly remind us that he is sufficient no matter what is happening. The best place I have seen to build up a person's faith shield is surrounding oneself with other believers of Jesus. Other Christ followers are taught to share each other's burdens and support and pray for one another. To love their neighbor. If you are finding yourself taking an onslaught of shots from Satan and you are beaten up, shield yourself by relying on other Christ followers to reinforce your faith in Jesus.

Next is the "Helmet of Salvation." The helmet protects the mind and thoughts. It symbolizes the assurance of salvation and the hope of eternal life, which guards believers against despair and deception. The great evangelist Billy Graham once said, "We cannot put it on; only Jesus puts salvation on us. When we put on the helmet of salvation, we put on Christ Himself. Christ protects not just our heads but our entire beings from spiritual death. To wear the helmet of salvation means to live every day focused on eternity and the promised future we have." Practically, what does this look like to a young Christian? Since it is a helmet, let us focus on that region of the body. It means to guard your thoughts and be mindful of what you allow into your mind. Do not allow toxicity to gain a foothold in your mind. Protect yourself from negative influences, doubts, and fears by focusing on the truths of God's Word and the security of your salvation. Sometimes, that means cutting out activities you participated in or people. For example, if you know that you are predisposed to overindulge in alcohol and lots of horrible things happen when you drink, it might behoove you to stay away from that demon. Protect yourself by doing different things that support God's kingdom and surrounding yourself with good Christian people. Get out of the strip club and take the bus to the Bible club! You need to know and be honest to utilize this armor properly. Know your negative predispositions with sins, turn away from them, and focus on Jesus. Throw away that negative influence or action and remember who God is and that He is love and has already saved you!

The final piece is the "Sword of the Spirit." The sword is the offensive weapon in the armor, representing the Word of God. It is used in spiritual battle to counter lies, temptations, and deception with the truth of God's Word. This is the piece that allows us to go after Satan. The other pieces were used for protection. This is how we take back what is rightfully ours. Practically, how we use the sword to fight Satan might surprise you. We take what we know and understand about the Word of God and put it into action. We go out and serve our communities in Jesus's name! We wield the sword by doing good deeds like feeding homeless people, volunteering in a battered women's shelter, or in some other charitable way. We let our actions of good be the weapon that fights Satan in this sin-filled world.

An incredibly worthy, honorable mention goes to prayer. Not mentioned as a physical piece of armor, prayer is emphasized as how believers stay connected to God, seeking his strength, wisdom, and guidance in all circumstances. Paul concludes in Ephesians 6:18–20 by urging believers to pray in the Spirit on all occasions, staying alert and persistent, and interceding not only for themselves but for all believers and him in spreading the gospel fearlessly. Overall, the armor of God represents the spiritual resources and protection God provides to his followers to stand firm against spiritual opposition and to advance his kingdom on Earth. So, pray constantly! Our greatest weapon against Satan and the power of darkness is communicating continually with our Father in Heaven.

Even with the various tips and suggestions to keep Satan from tripping us up, understand that he will eventually get a shot over the wall, and you will take a hit. What happens when he finally lands a punch? What happens when you sin now that you are a believer? How do you get yourself right? Luckily, the Bible teaches us about grace.

One thing the devil wants you not to believe in is the gift of grace that God freely gives you. Grace is a central concept that refers to the free and unmerited favor of God shown to humanity. It is a fundamental attribute of God's nature and character, expressed in his kindness, mercy, and forgiveness toward people. You cannot earn grace. It is a gift from God! Understand that God hates sin, but he loves you so much more. Ephesians 2:8–9 explains grace perfectly: "For it is by grace you have been saved, through faith—and this is not from yourselves, it is the gift of God—not by works so that no one can boast."

What is grace? It is the gift of forgiveness and reconciliation from God for your sins. God's grace in your life makes salvation possible through faith in Jesus Christ. God's grace is sufficient to meet all our needs and abounds even amid human weakness and sin. This understanding encourages believers to rely on God's grace in all circumstances. When a person scr*ws up, it is by God's grace that they can repent (turn away from) their sins and keep on living according to God's will. Yes, you will scr*w up occasionally, but luckily, all new believers are gifted grace so that they do not have to stay stuck in their sins. Grace is that tow cable to drag a person out of the mire and muck of sin the devil tries to keep us bogged down in. Praise Jesus for this gift of grace so that when we do trip, we are encouraged to stand up, dust ourselves off, and grow spiritually.

When you took that first breath after confessing that Jesus is your Lord and Savior, you became a target for Satan. You instantly became a light in a dark world. People are drawn to light, and Satan wants to dim your light to the point where no one can see it. Keep your light burning bright! Yes, you will sometimes falter and not live up to God's standards. It took Adam and Eve just three chapters into the Bible to fail. And Adam walked with God every single day! But know for a fact that God is going to take care of you no matter what. He sacrificed a couple of animals to clothe Adam and Eve, and he sent his one and only Son to die on the cross for your sins so that he can spend eternity with you!

God loves you! Satan can deceive, but he cannot win. Keep your eyes on Jesus! Your nose in the Bible. Surround yourself with other followers of Christ. Give back to your community. Don't just do the Great Commission but BE the Great Commission. Block the arrows that Satan fires at you every day. If one gets through and you sin, do not stop moving forward on the battlefield of life but repent and know that you are forgiven through the gift of grace. Satan is a worthy adversary, but he is an already defeated foe. Follow Jesus into battle and do your best to save others from the grip of the evil one.

Keep It Simple Step: Live with integrity in all areas of life, speaking truthfully and avoiding deceit. Jesus emphasized the importance of honesty and transparency. An easy example of living this out is to answer questions truthfully, no matter what you think the outcome might be. A frying pan to the head is still better than an eternity in hell getting poked by the devil.

> *Do not be wise in your own eyes; Fear the LORD and depart from evil. It will be a health to your flesh and strength to your ones.*
>
> *—Proverbs 3:7–8*

Fresh out of the Baptismal Pool

Read and journal on 2 Kings 5:14.

CHAPTER 3

CHURCH

Consequently, faith comes from hearing the message, which is heard through the word about Christ.

—Romans 10:17

My pastor, every week, usually ends his sermons by saying the same two things. He says he wants to "land the plane here" and asks, "So what?" The "land the plane here" usually implies I have fifteen minutes to belly to the drive-through or buffet for lunch. The "so what" question signifies the sermon's practical aspect that we just listened to. It is a question that turns what is in the Bible into a valuable life lesson for the believer or those still searching for Christ. This practicality is vital for the development of a new Christian. Often, it cannot be expounded enough in the service since so many people are at different stages in their walks with Christ. It is usually a very "general" type of answer so that it touches everyone in the pews. But for the new believer, simple, practical applications are essential. It is important to realize this after a Sunday sermon, even if you still feel lost or confused. The church worship service will always make you feel good, but after lunch, life tends to start hitting back at you. So, how do you make what the pastor discussed in a PowerPoint presentation applicable to your daily lives? How do you take a lesson or story from a 2,000-plus-year-old book and make it contemporary to your own life?

Gaining the most out of a sermon starts in the church's parking lot. Leave your issues in the car. It sounds easy, but it is essential. I do not know how often I was sitting in church listening to the pastor speak, while my mind wandering to issues at work or what I had to do after church or family drama. Put yourself in a clear mindset and be ready to absorb the knowledge and wisdom found in the teachings of the Word of God. Listen to Christian music, meditate, or pray. Practice discipline in your mind by forgetting the world's problems and focusing solely on the task at hand. Which is the absorption of the Word of God. Whatever you usually do to clear the anxiety of the day, do it! If what you do is go for a run in the morning, it looks like you will be waking up early on a Sunday. The mind should be devoid of any unnecessary distractions. Make yourself a vessel, so the Holy Spirit can move into you and fill you with Jesus.

This is, of course, easier said than done today. I am sure that since you started reading this chapter, your phone has gone off at least twice due to emails, text messages, or social media notifications. If you can, put your phone on silent, and before you walk into church, have a moment of honest prayer and reflection. In chapter 10, I will deeply detail prayer and reflection, but we will keep it simple for now. When you are sitting quietly in your car or on a bus before service, reflect on the glory of God and everything good He has provided you this week, month, year, or whatever timeframe you want. Put your mind in a state of gratitude. I know that your week or day might have been awful, but there is something that you can be grateful for. Find what it is and reflect on it before you walk into church.

After having a moment of reflection, go ahead and send up a prayer to the man upstairs! Let him know that you are ready to receive his teachings. I digress, but pray for whatever you want to; it is your prayer time. However, make sure you pray for the pastor and staff of the church. Pray that they are used as conduits for the gospel of Christ! Pray that the message is clear and concise and brings meaning and hope to yourself and everyone in the sanctuary. Pray that lives are changed because of the message of Jesus. Pray for the Holy Spirit to move into your church and bring forth the glory of God. Pray for your church because a church is not a building. Church is the body of believers together praising and following Christ Jesus.

I was a back-row Baptist for a while. I usually came in late and sat in the back row while the band was playing or about to be finished. Do not be me; it hindered my growth in so many ways. Be on time for church. Because if you are not, you will miss out on worship music, and you are only hindering yourself. When the worship leader calls for everyone to stand and sing praises, be ready and sing! No matter how off-key or tone-deaf you may be, sing like your life depends on it!

Music has a way of preparing the soul to be open to the Holy Spirit. Worship and sing praises while you are in church. Remember, in several parts of the Old Testament, King David sang and worshipped the Lord. If it were good enough for King David, it is good enough for you! Those hymnals and songs were written to prepare your mind and heart for the Word of God. Ensure you are there to capitalize on the worship time before the message. It is essential to your growth and ensures your mind is set on Jesus and his tremendous power.

Remember how hard you studied for a challenging high school or college class only to never use the information you were forced to take in? Information on subjects you thought were critical to your life at that time. Unlike "advanced statistics" or "philosophical ethics 110," sound biblical teaching is necessary information. Treat the church service like a challenging class. Listen intently while you are in the pew. Take notes that correspond with the verses that the pastor is going over. Write down questions that you have about the subject matter. After the service, ask or email the pastor or staff later for clarity. Treat the sanctuary like a classroom.

I did not understand this concept until later in my walk with Christ. I would look around the pews and wonder why that person brought a Bible and notebook to church. The Bible verse and message are written on the projector screen. Why would I need to write it down? Little did I realize that I was not listening until a couple of hours after church when someone asked me what the service was about. I could not remember! I might have remembered a Bible verse or something small, but the message did not stick. The travesty of it all is that I was usually talking to someone who was not saved and a believer in Christ. I missed a golden opportunity to possibly change a person's life simply because I did not write down notes on what the sermon was about. Once again, do not be me. Treat that sanctuary like a classroom a few days before a huge test!

<u>Halftime Scripture</u>: *They devoted themselves to the apostles' teaching and fellowship, to the breaking of bread and prayer.*

—Acts 2:42

Most of us grew up going to school and getting homework. Churches are not going to give members homework or a test. However, as I said in the previous chapter, Christians get tested by an adversary every single moment of the day. Just like in school, take your notes home and look over them. Write down the passages of the Bible that the pastor referenced in the presentation and reread them yourself. Study the word like you are studying for the SAT or another big test.

Take your sermon/Bible study notes and reference the passage with a trusted biblical commentary book. Why a biblical commentary book? These are written by several scholars and theologians who are experts on everything that has to do with that single book—the Bible. The commentary's authors explain in detail a specific passage's historical and cultural background. As the reader, you can understand Bible passages and sermons much better. The commentary also helps you realize the historical and societal significance and language used at the time a specific passage was written. It lets you understand the context since the Bible is a 2,000-plus-year-old book. A biblical commentary is a must-have for a follower of Christ in today's world to better understand the Bible.

What about at the end of the sermon when the pastor ties what he said with the bow of "the answer is Jesus"? What does that mean? You show up to church dealing with different life issues, and the pastor says the solution to your problem is Jesus. How is this practical in anyone's life? Remember that the Bible says that first, there was the word, and the word became flesh. The Word of God is the Bible. Your pastor refers to the Word of God when he says that the answer to whatever situation you are dealing with is Jesus. Please understand that I am not saying that Jesus cannot or will not do anything in the miracle department. On the contrary, I pray that he will perform miracles in your life. I am just speaking from a practical sense and experience as a Christ follower. The answer is always going to be Jesus. However, the Word of God, prayer, and the church will fix whatever ails you.

Jesus usually will not come down and write you a check so you can pay all your bills (maybe he will, but that has not ever happened to anyone I know), but the answer to your financial issues will be found in the Bible (the word). Jesus will not sit in a chair across from you, and a spouse who has marital issues like Dr. Phil, but the answer to having a great marriage is found in the Bible. When the pastor says the answer is Jesus, he implores the audience to look to the Bible for the answers to whatever situation they find themselves in. The most practical thing a new follower of Christ must do is read. Read the Bible. Cover to cover. If you do not understand something, grab a commentary that a pastor recommends and study like you have never learned before. If that does not work, ask a friend or staff member at the church. This is why discussing sermons with others is essential as well.

After the sermon is done and everyone has been dismissed, make time for fellowship with other church members. Discuss the sermon and what they thought about it. Discuss the sermon with other people in the church; you may gain different practical insights into what was being taught. They might have caught something crucial that you missed. Plus, it is a good icebreaker for people with a more introverted personality. If you do not have time afterward or feel awkward about asking folks about the sermon after church, do not fear! Write down your questions and bring them up to your small group or Bible study whenever you meet next. I am confident that if you have questions about something that was said during the sermon, other church members do as well.

When you are done networking and fellowshipping and have returned to the car, take a moment and pray. Just like you did before the service, reflect for a moment and praise God. Pray for God's guidance and strength to apply what you've learned. Ask him to help you grow spiritually and live according to his word. It is so important to show God the glory and let him know you realize how blessed you are. Remember that not everyone around the world can worship Jesus freely. But you are! You are blessed because you can learn and fellowship with other Christ followers in a safe and loving environment. Give God praise again before you head to lunch after church.

However, none of the things discussed in the chapter matter if you are not in the pews. Consistent attendance is crucial to getting the most out of your church service. I understand that everyone takes vacations or gets sick from time to time. But to get the most out of your church experience, you must be there every Sunday. There are so many benefits to being consistent in your attendance at church. Your time in the pews should feed you the spiritual nourishment you crave. It should create a sense of unity with other church members, which strengthens your relationship with God. Consistent church attendance is not a religious obligation but a source of spiritual enrichment, community support, and personal growth for believers. It provides a structured framework for worship, learning, fellowship, and service, ultimately helping individuals deepen their faith and love of Jesus Christ. Stop hitting the snooze button on Sunday morning and get to church!

Think of church like a class. The sermons might not have anything to do with your current season of life, but they will. Life seems to be a constant roller coaster of highs and lows, with climbs and descents in between. The only constant in life is change, and what we learn in the pews on Sunday morning will help all of us navigate the roller coaster ride of life. Treat church like a class; as a student, become a sponge, soaking in all the information you can!

Keep It Simple Step: Share your resources with those less fortunate through financial contributions, donating goods, or offering your time and skills. Generosity reflects a heart aligned with Jesus's teachings. An easy way to live this out is to go through your closet and find clothes that do not fit anymore or are maybe a little dated. Take them to a mission or homeless shelter.

> *My son, if you accept my words and store up my commands within you, turning your ear to wisdom and applying your heart to understanding—indeed, if you call out for insight and cry aloud for understanding, and if you look for it as for silver and search for it as for hidden treasure, then you will understand the fear of the Lord and find the knowledge of God. For the Lord gives wisdom; from his mouth comes knowledge and understanding. He holds success in store for the upright; he is a shield to those whose walk is blameless, for he guards the course of the just and protects the way of his faithful ones. Then you will understand what is right and just and fair—every good path. For wisdom*

will enter your heart, and knowledge will be pleasant to your soul. Discretion will protect you, and understanding will guard you.

—Proverbs 2:1–11

<u>Read and journal on Matthew 3:13–17.</u>

CHAPTER 4
THE BIBLE

In the beginning was the Word, and the Word was with God, and the Word was God.

—John 1:1

Theologians do a great job of taking simple subject matter and confusing the heck out of ordinary people. I am not saying that theology is an antiquated and unnecessary realm of study. On the contrary, theology is vital in answering significant questions posed by humans and answered by the Bible. Some of my favorite college courses were theology-based. I am just saying that for new followers of Christ, listening to charismatic allegories will only confuse you and minimize your spiritual impact. Remember that if you do not fully understand something, you cannot explain it entirely to the next person. It is essential to follow the KISS method of Christianity. KISS stands for "keep it simple, stupid." Typically, people start school in prekindergarten, not at a university. As a new Christ follower, I recommend you focus on the basics of studying and going about your day. What are the basics? The basics are found in the words of your Bible.

The pathway to practicality and foundational Christianity is in the pages of the Holy Bible. There are thousands of books written about the Bible, how to read the Bible, and devotions devoted to bringing out the "hidden" meanings of passages in the Bible. All of them are good and meaningful, but nothing compares to the actual words written in the Bible. Reading the Bible is the first practical step in becoming a warrior for Christ. Now, what is the most helpful way of reading the Bible? It seems there are more Bible study guides than people in the world! How does a person know where to start? I was also confused and overwhelmed in my spiritual journey in this study area. The Bible is a vast book. But it is an important book, and a cheat code is found in the back of most Bibles.

I started studying the Bible, beginning on page one of the book of Genesis, and read it cover to cover for over a year. When I got to the end of Revelation (the last book of the Bible), on the page next to it was a section of the Bible called "Read Your Bible Through in a Year." It was a daily breakdown of what to read in the morning and evening. Usually, it was a little bit of the New Testament in the morning and a little bit of the Old Testament in the evening. The Bible gave me a sensible and relevant breakdown of how to read it within the year. But I was hardheaded, read it cover to cover, and forgot and got confused with most of what I read. Do not be me!

Go into reading your entire Bible with a plan in place. Cover-to-cover reading can be an option, but it is not necessarily the best option. Utilize the "Read Your Bible Through in a Year" breakdown at the back. It breaks it down perfectly so that the reader is not overwhelmed. Remember, Satan is going to do everything he can to minimize your impact on the kingdom. If studying is a weakness for you, do not give in! A free, simple study guide is in the back of your Bible. Use it! Keep it simple! If you, by chance, have a version of the Bible that does not have that located in the back, search "Bible reading plans in a year" on the internet, and voila, you will have over four million options to choose from.

Another option for believers in reading the Bible is to break it down by specific genres or types of books within the Bible. The Bible contains various genres, including historical narratives, poetry, prophecy, and letters. Maybe it is hard to understand why Genesis reads so differently from the Song of Solomon. This is because they are of different styles or genres of books. Believers can also start their reading plan by focusing on significant sections of the Bible, like the gospels of Matthew, Mark, Luke, and John. By starting with the gospels, you are immediately learning about the life, teachings, and ministry of Jesus Christ. Another great place to start reading in the Bible is in Proverbs. Proverbs is an Old Testament book that has thirty-one chapters of very wise statements to help us live godly lives. The thirty-one chapters make it an easy-to-follow guide since most months have thirty-one days. Plus, none of the chapters are long, and it is an easy read! These are just a few tips I have used over the last decade and a half of being a Christian. Reading the Bible is a lifelong journey of spiritual growth and understanding. Enjoy the process and allow the Word of God to transform your life.

The question always arises about what translation or version of the Bible is best to learn from. Once again, I was just as overwhelmed when I started studying the Bible. Social media will make a person think that all the translations are different, proving they are not real and all that nonsense. Once again, that is Satan trying to cast doubt on your salvation. What translation of the Bible should you study from? I recommend a version of the Bible that you understand! If you barely passed your English literature classes in high school, you probably don't want to start with the King James Version (KJV) of the Bible. Nowadays, popular choices include the New International Version (NIV), English Standard Version (ESV), and New American Standard Bible (NASB). I was gifted a New King James Version (NKJV) by my ex-wife many years ago, and it has never left my side. It is a personal preference based on you as an individual. I highly recommend asking your pastor what version of the Bible he bases his sermons on. That way, what you learn in the pews is like what you read Monday to Saturday on your own.

Regardless of your Bible type or study guide, the Bible will arguably be your best tool in your everyday walk with Christ. It is the lynchpin that everything else in your walk with Christ falls upon. Use it and study it like your life depends on it. Because, in all actuality, it does. The Bible is the most important book ever written and should be the foundation document of your life.

But I understand it can be the most intimidating book you have ever seen. A book like the Bible is so powerful and filled with so much knowledge that maybe Satan is using that intimidation to keep you from learning. I want to encourage you if you are feeling this way. If you feel overwhelmed or intimidated by the Bible, know that your heart is in the correct place to receive all its excellent knowledge. Remember that Proverbs 1 says, "The fear of the Lord is the beginning of knowledge." Fear is seen here as respect, and you are probably intimidated because your heart knows that what is found in the Bible is life-changing! Embrace the fear, and as the old saying goes, eat the elephant one bite at a time.

If you are feeling overwhelmed or at a place where you do not understand what is going on or why it matters, there are plenty of options to help you know what you just read. Utilize a biblical commentary to assist you with understanding. Write it down and ask a question for your Bible study leader. Pray to the Lord Almighty about it. Or what most 21st-century people do—google it! Most people are wary of the validity of everything found online, and I agree. However, a quick internet search regarding a passage could clarify some confusion that a person may have with the Bible. Information is accessible on your phone or device. Do not get discouraged when reading. Get creative and utilize available resources to help you understand God's word.

> <u>Halftime Scripture</u>: *All Scripture is God-breathed and is useful for teaching, rebuking, correcting and training in righteousness, so that the servant of God may be thoroughly equipped for every good work.*
>
> *—2 Timothy 3:16–17*

Have reverence for your Bible. I may lose a lot of tech-savvy folks with this statement, but I will suggest it anyway. Ensure your primary Bible is a physical handheld book. Not an app or a Bible found on a device like a tablet or phone. I mean, the Bible is Holy. It is the inspired Word of God. It deserves to be respected. Do you think it is appropriate for your Bible, the inspired Word of God, to be on the same device that you have your social media and dating apps on? The inspired and infallible Word of God has no place on a device next to the app you use to order pizza from. Remember that fear (respect) of the Lord is the beginning of knowledge, so it would behoove you to keep your Bible separate and hallowed. Respect your Bible. Please keep it in a safe and dry place, easily accessible to everyone in the house. Never put your Bible on the floor! A tattered, messy, and used Bible in a person's hand is the most potent weapon for doing good on the planet. It should be held in higher regard than an app on a phone that you will take into the bathroom and play games on.

To continue with that same train of thought, have a dedicated space or an area to read your Bible. I am not saying you should not read your Bible outside in the car or wherever necessary. Your study spot is up to you. However, having a quiet, dedicated place to hold and study your Bible is important. Seek out a corner of your home where you and your Bible can be. Make sure it is calm, away from distractions, and has excellent lighting to make it easier to read. Build your Bible-studying corner however you want. Just ensure that it is in the best place for you. In the previous chapter, I touched briefly on the act of worship before the sermon. Make sure you are in the same mind frame of prayer so that you can receive the Word of God in full and without distractions. Where you read your Bible matters.

What is the best way to get into a mind frame of worshiping to study your Bible? The best way to begin your Bible study is with a simple prayer. Praying will prepare your heart and mind to focus on God. To give thanks and get whatever is on your heart off your chest. It is the best way to start your study session because it focuses first on what is important: your relationship with Jesus Christ. Do not think that you will need a long-drawn-out prayer that would make the cardinals in the Vatican jealous at five in the morning. I completely understand if your brain is not at its best before the effects of your first cup of joe hit. God knows what is in your heart. Just make it a simple prayer and dig into the Word of God.

When you read your Bible matters as well. The time of day you read your Bible should be when you can devote all of yourself to it. It is often suggested to read the Bible in the morning. Make it the first thing that you do. This suggestion has some scriptural backing to it, too. Psalm 5:3 says, "My voice You shall hear in the morning, O Lord; In the morning, I will direct it to You, And I will look up." The Bible has several passages that point to the benefits of devoting your mornings to the Lord. However, we live in a bustling world nowadays. I know that not everyone starts their day at six in the morning. I recommend bookending your days with reading from the Bible and prayer. Read a little in the morning and read a little before bedtime. That way, you start and end your day with the Word of God. Is it always practical or feasible? No. However, you make time for things that are important to you. Try it out, and make time to read and study the Bible.

Five minutes of reading the Bible daily will have a much more significant impact on your life than reading the Bible for five hours every third Tuesday of the month, every September 12th, or whatever random day you choose. Consistency is key in studying the Bible. Make it a routine. No matter what time of day works for you, ensure your nose is in that book, even if only for a few minutes. Those few minutes of study will significantly impact the other twenty-three hours and fifty-seven minutes of your day. It is the inspired and infallible Word of God. Perfect in every way. It should have a powerful impact on your life, even in small doses.

It has been said that your relationship with Jesus Christ is profoundly personal, but your growth with him is not. You need other Christians in your life to grow. This fact is also true of how you study the Word of God. A tremendous help for me in understanding the Bible better was when I joined a Bible study group. Your church may have a different name for it. Some call it "Sunday school" or "small groups." But they are all the same thing in general. It is a place outside the worship service on Sunday morning where you can engage in discussions with others who are also studying the Bible. These groups exist to provide different perspectives and insights that deepen your understanding of what you read in the Bible. You can ask questions about things that do not make sense to you. Learn from more seasoned or mature Christians. These small Bible study groups are excellent places to compare ideas you have discovered when performing your Bible study. These small groups also tend to have a curriculum or lesson plan to guide you in what to read in the Bible during the week. Becoming part of a Bible study group is crucial in helping you understand the Bible.

The Bible is more than just a book. It is a vital source of spiritual nourishment, guidance, and encouragement for everyone who opens its pages. It offers wisdom for navigating life's challenges, reveals the character of God, and provides the foundation for faith in Jesus Christ. As you read the Bible more consistently, you will discover truths that resonate deep within your soul. You will find strength in its promises and experience the transformative power of God's word. Embrace the Bible as your companion and guide. Let it shape your heart, mind, and spirit as you grow in your relationship with Jesus Christ. The Bible is life-changing, and its powers are incomprehensible. Pick up the Bible and read it as often as you can!

Keep It Simple Step: Study the Bible and understand its teachings. Apply biblical principles to your daily life, seeking wisdom and guidance from God's word. An excellent way to remember this is to keep your Bible next to your coffee pot in the kitchen. You can read scripture while you wait for the coffee to be made.

> *Hear, my children, the instruction of a father, and give attention to know to understand; For I give you sound doctrine: Do not forsake my law.*
>
> *—Proverbs 4:1–2*

Read and journal on Mark 16:16.

CHAPTER 5
SMALL GROUPS

Wherefore comfort yourselves together, and edify one another, even as also ye do.

—1 Thessalonians 5:11

Vulnerability is scary. Meeting new people is not always everyone's cup of tea. Society is more closed off than ever in 2024. How do we fix this issue? By looking at the past. People used to enjoy being around one another, not glued to their phones. New Christians need to get over themselves and trust God. One of the most significant issues people have after accepting Christ is finding their place in the church. Satan knows this, too. He knows that being a new Christian is like being in a new high school after moving. The enemy knows that you are probably anxious about being around new people. You may think, what if these people don't like me? What if I can't make friends in church, of all places? He wants to get into your head because it benefits him and his sick and twisted game of manipulation. He wants to minimize your growth and impact, which will cause fewer people to be saved in Christ. A new Christ follower must be bold and search for a group of people within the church who will nurture and support their growth. That is why it is so crucial for a new Christ follower to join a small group immediately after being saved and baptized.

What is a small group, you ask? It is a group of similar individuals within a church who come together during the week to learn the Bible and support each other in their walks with Christ. It resembles the model of the earlier church. Small groups meeting in a home or anywhere outside the sanctuary to get to know and care about one another. A small group is where you can ask the questions that bother you. Where you can be vulnerable to your peers and not feel judged. It is a group of strangers for whom, over time, Christ becomes a family.

Why are small groups important? Small groups are essential because all Christ's followers need to be loved and nurtured. New Christians are starting a brand-new life. In John 3:3, Jesus tells Nicodemus, "Most assuredly, I say to you, unless one is born again, he cannot see the kingdom of God." Think of this in a literal sense. Without a family to take care of it, a newborn baby would die of exposure probably a day or two after birth. I know that doesn't sound warm-hearted, but it is true. This is why you need to find fellowship and family within the church. A baby needs a family to take care of it, feed it, and nurture it to grow and reach its full potential. A small group is that family for a new Christian. The worship service on Sunday morning is like a classroom. A small group is where followers of Christ go to be vulnerable and support one another in their daily struggles while also learning and delving deeper into the Bible and exploring their faith in Christ. These small groups are crucial to the growth and development of a new believer in Christ.

Where do you find these small groups? Most churches nowadays know the importance of small groups and have dedicated programs and schedules. Group leaders are well-educated, vetted, and placed in similar groups of people to keep the focus on Christ. If you go to a smaller church, usually, there are separate Bible studies that you can attend outside of worship service. They are typically broken down by age group and gender. The best thing to do is reach out to one of the pastors in your church and ask to join one. You must be inquisitive and ask questions to grow your relationship with Christ.

Be bold and ask to join a small group. If your church does not offer a small group that aligns with where you are at in life, ask to create one. Maybe none of the small groups available involve something relevant to you. That is okay. It may mean that God wants you to lead. I can almost guarantee that you are not the only person in your church who has your interests or is in the same stage or season of life as you are. Reach out and try it. With God at the center, nothing can fail. However, being a small group leader is a lot of work, so please start small. The best leaders were first followers. Nine times out of ten, there will be a small group already set up that you can join and be comfortable in.

Not all people get along with or are at the same stage of life as other people. This is the biggest hurdle most people must overcome by becoming part of a small group. Many churches have thought about this and have all types of small groups. They are based on various intangibles like age, family structure, occupation, and geographic location. There are also small groups of people with similar interests outside of the Bible but who incorporate Christ into what they enjoy doing. For example, I have been a part of a small group of men who like to golf. We would play nine holes and meet in the clubhouse afterward for fellowship and Bible study. It was a lot of fun! A person is more inclined to stick with something if they feel comfortable and have fun doing it, so make sure you get in where you fit in with a small group.

As a new follower of Christ, you probably wonder precisely what you are signing up for when you attend a small group. It can be a nerve-racking experience. At first, I dreaded attending small groups. I am introverted, so this was probably my biggest hurdle and stunted my growth as a Christ follower. I worked all day, and now I had to go and be uncomfortable in someone else's house. I had to pretend to enjoy being with others when I just wanted to sit at home and pet my dog. Looking back, I realized that Satan just wanted me to stay home so that I could not reap the benefits that true Christian friendship gives you. It was not until I was at my wit's end that I realized how important it is to have people in your corner. Good, solid people who have your back, not because of the same last name or similarity in a bloodline but because of the blood shed by Jesus Christ. Do not be me! Take a deep breath and take the first step to your new extended family. But what should you expect at a small group meeting? Let's dive into what to expect so that it will not shock you.

Let's first look at the hierarchy of a traditional small group. There is usually a group leader. Sometimes, there is an assistant in case the leader gets sick, has work or regular life, and cannot do it. That leader is typically vetted by the church. Often, they are an elder, deacon, deaconess, or someone in good standing in the church. Small groups do not just pop up out of nowhere. They are sponsored by the church so that nothing nefarious is taught or goes on. This leader usually has a lesson plan, like a teacher, and they plan the evening curriculum-wise. Next is arguably the most important person—the host of the small group. This is the person whose home everyone is meeting in. If anyone has ever thrown a party, you understand the stress associated with this position. The host will generally be the one to let everyone know all the intangibles of the get-together so that everyone can have a great evening. Depending on the demographic, the small group will dictate the rest of the major players in a successful group. I have attended small groups where babysitters could watch the kids so the adults could talk. If this is the case, make sure you have a few extra bucks to tip the babysitter because, to be honest, those kids can get rowdy.

> <u>Halftime Scripture</u>: *But if we walk in the light, as he is in the light, we have fellowship with one another, and the blood of Jesus, his Son, purifies us from all sin.*
>
> *—John 1:7*

When you signed up for a small group, you probably did so because of a commonality in geographic location or demographics. For example, you are a married mother of two, and you see a small group that caters to married couples with kids close to your house. This small group might be a winner-winner chicken dinner for you and your husband. I hope you were invited to a small group of people you have already made friends with so that it is not entirely awkward for you. Christians should always be inviting and looking to comfort others, so hopefully, this was the case for you.

Often, you will see what the small group will be going over curriculum-wise, like a book club. The curriculum may be based on a particular book of the Bible. It might be a book written by another author explaining something interesting in the Bible. Maybe it is a class or workshop on strengthening Christian marriages or prayer. The possibilities are endless, but they should always focus back on our savior, Jesus Christ. On a side note, the small group leader will let you know if you need any other books or items to ensure you get the most out of the small group. Make sure that the curriculum that the small group is going over is relevant and exciting to you. You are meant to learn something in your small group. Ensure that it is in line with the stage of life you are in. You would not want to join a small group for older women who golf if you are a twenty-five-year-old man who likes to skateboard. You will probably not be inclined to go if the topic and people are unattractive. You will miss out on a golden opportunity to become a part of an extended family of Christ followers. So, make sure you are in the correct group for *you*.

In my experience, prayer is a cornerstone of small group participation. Leaders often invite members to share their prayer requests, fostering a sense of community and support. This is usually done toward the end of the meeting, before everyone wraps up. Be prepared to engage in prayer frequently during your time in a small group. The impact of your prayers and how much they help will depend on your openness and willingness to share with the group.

Regarding prayer time, there are usually two different types of people at these meetings: those with no filters and those with perfect lives that fit social media. People with the perfect lives fit for social media will usually have superficial prayer requests, typically never about themselves, because they are perfect people or at least want to appear that way. These are usually the people with the most disturbing stuff, but that is another topic. The other kind of people are those who use prayer request time as an inexpensive alternative to years of therapy they should probably be enrolled in. They emotionally vomit and take up most of the group leader's time. I would sit stunned at the difference in everyone's personalities and wonder if these prayer requests ever worked. Let me tell you, they most certainly do.

I remember vividly one night at a men's group Bible study, an older gentleman said that his sister was in hospice with stage four cancer. We all prayed for her and the family, and the meeting ended sadly. A couple of weeks later, on our group chat, the old man messaged that his sister was cured and moved back into her home.

I was astonished. When we saw the older man at the next meeting, we were delighted to discover his sister was miraculously healed. Did our group prayer help? The Bible answers in Matthew 18:19–20, "Again, I say to you that if two of you agree on earth concerning anything that they ask, it will be done for them by My Father in heaven. For where two or three are gathered in My name, I am there in the midst of them." Utilize your prayer time for one another in your small group. Be open and honest and pray for what matters. Miracles through prayer do happen!

Food is terrific and brings people together. Expect to be well-fed in a small group. In a traditional small group setting, food is usually the centerpiece of the evening. Some small groups have theme nights for dinners; some buy pizza or takeout; all are great options. Usually, the host will decide what the menu will entail. Some will ask to do a potluck-style dinner. Some will ask for cash to go and buy food and make it themselves. Some might meet up at a restaurant before or after the small group. The host family decides the food. Just be prepared to eat. Also, be ready to dust off your grandmother's cookbook and learn to make some covered dishes or casseroles. Nothing says Jesus loves you like a covered dish casserole. If you cannot cook for whatever reason, have no fear! Picking up something premade at a supermarket will be great, too. Often, it is preferred. As you read the Bible, notice how important food was to Jesus. He was always teaching and having dinners with people. Food and fellowship are good things that bring joy to everyone. That is what small groups are trying to emulate. Food and fellowship go hand in hand with small groups.

Fellowship is a large part of small groups. What is fellowship? A fellowship is an association of people who share one's interests and like to hang out together. Luckily, if you are in a Christian small group, you already have something in common with everyone else: Jesus Christ. He is the lynchpin of everything, isn't he? However, it is necessary to point out that people are imperfect. Especially folks who say they are Christ followers. No one is perfect except Jesus, but sometimes, some people do not mesh well with others. Make sure you enjoy being around the people in your small group.

You should feel excited to do life with the people in your small group. You should feel supported and want to help others in your circle. If that is not happening, then maybe that is not the group for you. If you do not feel comfortable in several groups, the issue might be you, and some introspection and therapy might help. But it would be best to enjoy the folks you are with genuinely. Hopefully, your relationship blossoms and you all get to do outings or trips together.! It is perfectly acceptable to "test drive" different small groups. Make sure you always feel comfortable and enjoy being around the people in your group. The growth you will experience while a part of these small groups is undeniable and critical to your walk with Christ.

Keep It Simple Step: Offer to pray with friends, family members, or colleagues who are going through difficult times. Praying together builds community and demonstrates reliance on God. Whenever you hear that someone is going through something or has terrible news to report, tell that person that you will pray for them and then remember to do it. It's funny, but I have even had atheist friends who accept my offers to pray for them.

> *He who walks with the wise men will be wise, but the companion of fools will be destroyed.*
>
> *—Proverbs 13:20*

Read and journal on Acts 8:12–17.

CHAPTER 6
MENTORSHIP

But as for you, speak the things which are proper for sound doctrine: that the older men be sober, reverent, temperate, sound in faith, in love, in patience; the older women likewise, that they are respectful in behavior, not slanderers, not given to much wine, teachers of good things—that they admonish the young women to love their husbands, to love their children, to be discreet, chaste, homemakers, good, obedient to their husbands, that the word of God may not be blasphemed. Likewise, encourage the young men to be sober-minded, all things showing yourself to be a pattern of good works; in doctrine showing integrity, reverence, incorruptibility, sound speech that cannot be condemned, that one who is an

> *opponent may be ashamed, having nothing evil to say of you. Exhort bondservants to be obedient to their masters, to be well pleasing in all things, not answering back, not pilfering, but showing all good fidelity, that they may adorn the doctrine of God our Savior in all things.*
>
> *—Titus 2:1–10*

No one is self-made. I have noticed in my thirty-eight years on Earth that successful people usually hang out with other successful people. They tend to find people in positions they want to attain. For example, a friend of mine is a wildly successful entrepreneur. He went out and found other entrepreneurs at Chamber of Commerce meetings and had coffee with all of them. The entrepreneurial knowledge he attained from those trips to a coffee shop was immense for his development. Successful people are curious about these people, and they go out boldly and befriend them. The same is true for followers of Christ. Finding a mentor is critical to the development of a new Christian.

Mentorship is also deeply rooted in the Bible. Numerous examples are found in both the Old and New Testaments. One Old Testament example is in Deuteronomy

Chapter 34—the relationship between Moses and Joshua. In that book, Moses mentored Joshua and prepared him to take over for him after he died. To carry the torch and fulfill God's plan. Moses guided, encouraged, and passed on leadership responsibilities to him over several years.

Another example in the Old Testament is found in 2 Kings Chapter 2 with Elijah and Elisha. Elijah was a mentor and trained Elisha to become a prophet of God. The relationship shows us how important it is to impart wisdom and spiritual insight to another person. The fantastic thing is that Elisha does not ask for fame or notoriety but for a double portion of Elijah's spirit. That way, he can have an even more significant impact on God's kingdom.

In the New Testament, a prime example of mentorship is Jesus's mentoring of his disciples. The gospels are filled with teachings and wisdom that Jesus passed on to his disciples. His mentorship was perfect. He taught, guided, nurtured, encouraged, and corrected these men for three years. Jesus's actions laid the groundwork for Christianity to flourish into what it is today.

The final New Testament example of mentorship in the Bible that I will touch upon is the relationship between Paul and Timothy. In Paul's letter to Timothy, Paul describes him as his "true son in the faith" and discusses how they have spent so much time together. This shows the investment that Paul made in Timothy.

Paul's letters to Timothy give the reader a glimpse of the advice, teaching, and personal encouragement needed to lead a church. For lack of a better term, all these examples illustrate people training their replacements. Admittedly, they were trained very well since the church has thrived throughout millennia.

What should you be looking for in a mentor? When I checked into my first command in the navy, I remember being assigned another more seasoned sailor. I was told never to leave his back pocket and learn everything I could from him. I can say that I was blessed because I am still in touch and have incredible respect for that person twenty-plus years later. Not all my fellow younger sailors were as lucky as me, though. Some were given mentors who did not have the most admirable qualities. Unlike career mentors, a Christian mentor must possess specific hard-to-find qualities. Christian mentors should exhibit spiritual maturity, a consistent prayer life, and a lifestyle that reflects Christ-like values and principles. They should also know scripture, compassion, patience, and integrity and be accountable. These are just a few that I have found helpful.

Have you ever heard of the Billy Graham rule? It is a rule that the great evangelist Billy Graham had regarding the opposite sex. Billy Graham would not ride in cars or dine with a single woman one-on-one. He did not want anyone to doubt his fidelity in any situation. While this may seem strange or sexist today, it is a good rule to follow when choosing a Christian mentor. Find a mentor of the same gender. Men need to learn from other men, and women need to learn from other women. No matter what society will have you believe, there are differences between men and women. Plus, men know how men feel, and women know how women respond about specific subjects. It just makes sense, and it keeps away ideas of affairs or inappropriate sexual relationships occurring.

> <u>Halftime Scripture:</u> *You then, my son, be strong in the grace of Christ Jesus. And the things you have heard me say in the presence of many witnesses entrust to reliable people who will also be qualified to teach others.*
>
> *—2 Timothy 2:1–2*

Mentors need to be older in faith than you. More seasoned in life as a Christ follower. Notice that I did not say older as in age but older in faith. I have met many younger people who are leading pastors of churches or deacons. This is one of those situational authority-type instances where the old, gray-haired fellow in the suit is not always the one you should be taking advice from about Christ. It may be the young guy in skinny jeans who is very learned in Christ. However, in most cases, those older people are usually wiser and make for excellent mentors since they have already been through the wringer of life. Keep your eyes open when you are at church. God will equip you by putting the correct people in front of you. It may be a seasoned church member you would never have thought you needed.

Usually, churches have a deacon staff or elders who are already vetted by the church and go through classes to teach the word and lead. These people are an excellent place to start when searching for a mentor. Have coffee or lunch with them. See if you have anything in common with each other. See if you click. Make sure you respect that person and what they stand for. Also, remember that mentors are people, too. People are not always perfect, so give grace to those in leadership positions. Bible studies are also a great place to befriend mentors. Usually, people who attend Bible studies have similar interests. I have been a part of an entrepreneurial Bible study and met a great friend and mentor through that. This friend had a successful business and was on fire for Jesus, so from my viewpoint, it was a win-win situation. Mentors are available in the church. It is merely a factor of vulnerability and asking questions to find one.

Make sure to let people know that you are looking for a Christian mentor. Lots of churches have mentorship programs already. For instance, my church has a discipleship program that kicks off in the fall each year. Mentors are already preselected, and mentees who sign up are selected. This provides oversight in the mentorship process by the church. Talk to a pastor on staff. More than likely, he knows someone who has a similar background or some form of commonality to you and can act as a mentor matchmaker. Be prepared to leave your comfort zone when you are first introduced. Give it time. If your heart and intentions are good, God will provide an excellent mentor to you. A strong soldier in faith!

Remember that the relationship between mentors and mentees is very different from other types of relationships you encounter. Mentors are there to guide and push you to a specific goal. Usually, it is a goal that they have already attained. That is why mentors are found in corporate America. These mentors can share their success with people who want to take their place on the totem pole when they retire. Understand that your relationship is not going to be a normal friend-zone relationship. A good mentor is going to push you so that you can grow. He will call you out when you are not hitting the mark. A mentor is really like a goal-specific coach. It can be a lot of work, but it is worth it. Jesus is worth it! You are worth it.

Accountability is critical in this mentor-mentee relationship. I remember when I first started in the discipleship program at my church and was paired up with my mentor. He was great and gave me a lot of thought-provoking questions at the start of the month that I would have to answer and discuss with him at our next luncheon or coffee. Sometimes, I would get sidetracked, miss a meeting, or forget to do Bible study. When I forgot to do a task, it sucked because I felt terrible about it. He took time out of his busy schedule to disciple me, and I missed the mark. Put your best foot forward and give it your best when being mentored. Be accountable to them; you will learn so much and experience exponential growth in Jesus Christ.

My mother always told me that it always takes two to tango. There cannot be an on-fire mentor with a cold mentee. As a mentee, there are a few things you need to make sure that you are doing as well to ensure a great and rewarding relationship for both of you. The mentee plays an active role in that they must be willing to learn and grow. They must be able to apply the mentor's teachings to their life. This willingness to learn is foundational to the success of both parties. Open and honest communication is vital to the relationship as well. The mentee should feel open to discussing everything with their mentor. This openness allows for more meaningful conversations and allows the mentor to be more effective in guidance. Mentees must be committed to the process, ensuring they meet and follow through with agreed-upon goals and actions. Trust is tremendous for both the mentee and the mentor. It is the bedrock that the relationship is built on. Hopefully, you will feel very comfortable quickly so that you can begin to reap the benefits of this biblically inspired relationship.

Several benefits of spiritual growth within a church happen when churches adopt a robust mentorship program. One by-product of an effective mentorship program within a church is the nontraditional bonding of people in a community. It is not every day that a twenty-five-year-old man befriends an eighty-year-old man. These connections build a network of support and encouragement through the different generations of church members. This generational bridge promotes a sense of community that helps strengthen the overall body of believers. Another aspect not usually discussed is church discipline, highlighted and strengthened through mentorship. Mentorship encourages accountability and responsibility in the mentees' and mentors' spiritual journeys. By holding each other accountable, both can help ensure that they live out their faith in a way that honors God and aligns with the Bible.

The church needs to recognize the importance of mentorship. Elders in the faith need to be open to reaching out and mentoring the next generation of church leaders. As a new follower of Christ, you need to reach out and seek wisdom from a mentor. In all actuality, elders in the church should be looking for mentees just as much as you are looking for a mentor. The benefits to both parties and the church are immense. Mentorship is a powerful tool for the development of both parties involved. In building relationships based on trust, compassion, and mutual respect, mentors and mentees can experience overwhelming growth in their walks with Christ. Like with all relationships, some issues may arise, but the benefits of mentoring far outweigh the difficulties. With mentorship, individuals can deepen their relationship with God, strengthen their faith, and contribute to a supportive and lasting community of Christ followers.

Keep It Simple Step: Show empathy and kindness to everyone you encounter, regardless of their background or circumstances. Compassion was central to Jesus's ministry. Do not judge a book by its cover. Every time you meet someone, try to find something unique about them. You never know what type of lives people live until you open and chat with them. Even if all you have time for is a simple, "Hello, nice weather we are having" conversation. Be kind and talk to everyone. That kindness could, in turn, benefit you in the end. Remember, showing empathy and compassion is not just lovely; it's a fundamental part of being a follower of Christ.

Instruct a wise man, and he will be yet wiser: teach a just man, and he will increase in learning.

—Proverbs 9:9.

Fresh out of the Baptismal Pool

Read and journal on Romans 6:3–4.

CHAPTER 7
SERVICE AND VOLUNTEERISM

Bear one another's burdens, and so fulfill the law of Christ.

—*Galatians 6:2*

Have you ever helped at a volunteer event? Maybe it was for a company you worked with or to satisfy some community service requirement for college. How did you feel after it? Probably a little tired but also accomplished, full of purpose, joyful, and maybe a little pride sprinkled in amongst some other feelings. Take those feelings and combine them with the kingdom of

God. Just think about how you will feel when you serve within your church. While every part of your walk with Jesus will cause you to grow, serving and volunteerism can be seen as an accelerant to the fire within you for Christ. It may also show you what your true God-given gifts and purpose are. Serving with the church is not just about helping others; it's about finding your place in the community and growing into the person God intended you to be.

One of the most significant biblical examples of service and volunteering can be found in the Old Testament story of Nehemiah. I will do my best to summarize it. Here is a man who was influential to the king of Persia as a cupbearer. But when finding out that Jerusalem's walls still lay in ruins, he felt moved to do something. He asked the king to leave his posh lifestyle in the royal court to rebuild the walls around Jerusalem. Nehemiah was granted his request. However, when he arrived in Jerusalem, he received a lot of opposition from neighboring enemies, who attacked him and his workers. Nehemiah faced internal challenges, too, including complaints of oppression among the Jews and economic hardships. In essence, many trials occurred, and he had to overcome them. His leadership and trust in God completed the walls in just fifty-two days. Nehemiah selflessly acted and volunteered when he heard the call from God. What he did is no different than what you will do when volunteering and serving at church.

I will paint with a broad stroke here, but all churches need volunteers to operate smoothly and be the hands and feet of God. Getting engaged in a church volunteer group is simple. Many churches have programs where you can try out different sectors of the church without altogether buying into something you do not like. Consider your gifts, what you enjoy and dislike, and look for opportunities. Then try it out. You have nothing to lose, and in many cases, you will meet some great people with similar interests.

For instance, you can try out in the nursery if you like kids. If you love singing, try out for the choir or band. If you are outgoing, look for the hospitality department, pass out coffee, or help new people get checked into the kids' ministry. If you are an introvert like me, I always enjoyed the parking lot ministry because it was outside and I did not have to talk to anyone, but I still had to help.

Now remember that with service and volunteerism, attitude is everything. You "get" to volunteer. You do not "need" or "have" to volunteer. If you ever feel like you need or have to volunteer, you feel guilt, not joy. I have both seen and felt this difference personally. Pastors are not perfect; they need you to help run the church, so they tend to get burned-out. The trick to not getting burned-out is found within the church's people. Try to get as many people as possible involved in serving.

Spread the work and spread the joy. If you feel burned-out, it is probably not from greeting people as part of the hospitality team. It is perhaps due to outside-of-church stressors. Work, family, and finances are prevalent stressors, to name a few. These stressors are very real and need to be dealt with so that you can get back into the game of service. Be honest with yourself, your situation, and your feelings. Be upfront with your pastors and serving teams. Let them know what you are going through, how you feel, and that you need a break. Serving others should be done with a joyful heart. Not a guilty one.

How does serving help you grow as a Christian? The first answer is that Jesus Christ calls us to serve others. As followers of Christ, we are constantly trying to be like him. Jesus did not go around telling people to pay homage to him. On the contrary, Christ washed people's feet. He ate dinner and hung out with tax collectors and prostitutes. He healed the lame and sick no matter what the instance. The Savior of the world was helping blind people see, so I am pretty sure you can pour a cup of coffee for a new person being introduced to your church one Sunday morning a month. One of the leadership qualities that I love about Jesus is that he practiced what he preached. Especially when it came to service and volunteerism. Our goal as followers of Christ is to be more like Jesus, and Jesus served others, so it is a beautiful place to start.

<u>Halftime Scripture</u>: *Is not this the kind of fasting I have chosen: to loose the chains of injustice and untie the cords of the yoke, to set the oppressed free and break every yoke? Is it not to share your food with the hungry and shelter the poor wanderer—when you see the naked, to clothe them, and not to turn away from your flesh and blood? Then your light will break forth like the dawn, and your healing will quickly appear; your righteousness will go before you, and the glory of the Lord will be your rear guard. Then you will call, and the Lord will answer; you will cry for help, and he will say: Here am I. If you do away with the yoke of oppression, with the pointing finger and malicious talk, and if you spend yourselves on behalf of the hungry and satisfy the needs of the oppressed, then your light will rise in the darkness, and your night will become like the noonday. The Lord will always guide you; he will satisfy your needs in a sun-scorched land and strengthen your frame. You will be like a well-watered garden, like a spring whose waters never fail.*

—Isaiah 58:6–11

Another way serving helps a Christ follower grow is that it allows you to use God-given gifts purposefully. I do not know many people who find fulfillment and joy as a shill in a corporate office downtown. However, that same shill could belt out hymnals like Whitney Houston and positively impact the church. That person could use that God-given voice to pull on the heartstrings of someone in the audience and allow themselves to feel the Holy Spirit move them toward submitting to Christ. Maybe you cannot sing, but you love teaching. Just think how many children you will impact by teaching them essential stories of the Bible, exposing these young people to Christ, and allowing the Holy Spirit to plant a seed in them. That seed may not bloom for a while, but your love of teaching helped plant it, and one day, it will grow.

Serving allows you to form relationships with fellow believers, fostering a sense of community and accountability within the church. When you volunteer to serve in whatever capacity you decide at church—worship team, hospitality team, production team, teaching team, security team, to name a few—you will meet some great people. These people probably have interests similar to yours. Serving is a great way to meet new people who are followers of Jesus Christ. Strengthening your base of friends with those who follow Jesus is essential. Serving alongside them is a fantastic way to meet new friends, make lifelong friends, and build a church family.

Serving requires putting others' needs before your own, fostering humility and a servant-hearted attitude, which aligns with Christ's teachings. Almost everyone whom you will come in contact with serving on Sunday morning has a full-time job. They probably have a family and bills to pay, just like you. They probably also would like to be on a tropical vacation, but instead, they use their precious time to volunteer to serve others at the church. Think about that sacrifice for a minute. Time is the one thing we cannot get more of, and these brothers and sisters volunteering alongside you give up their free time for Jesus Christ. This is the most transparent definition of practically putting God first that I can see. To sacrifice your time to expand the kingdom of God is what Jesus was talking about when he gave us the Great Commission. Serving puts yourself and your interests on the back burner so God can take center stage.

Engaging in acts of service helps develop compassion and empathy toward others, mirroring Christ's love for all people. Anytime you work in customer service, you will encounter people from every walk of life. Those who are well-off, those who are struggling, and those who are depressed—basically name any emotion and use it as an adjective to describe the people that you will meet. When you volunteer and serve, you treat everyone with the same respect that Jesus offered others. No matter what those people have going on. You may converse with someone while you serve them a cup of coffee. That conversation might help bring that person out of a depressive episode or something. In serving, you practice compassion, which can have a massive impact on everyone you meet. Little things matter; by serving, you bring Christ's love to someone who may not even realize it. Everyone is fighting a battle that comes into church. Your small act of service can be the extra bit needed to help that individual fight whatever demons they are currently battling.

Many roles in church service involve leadership responsibilities, offering opportunities to develop and refine leadership skills in a Christian context. The next chapter details how, in serving, you are growing as a leader in Christ. Jesus flipped the idea of leadership over two thousand years ago. Servant leadership is the name of his game and is the best type of leadership there is. Great leaders serve and make those under them better. When you volunteer, you put others ahead of yourself, and thereby, do leadership exactly how Christ intended. In a practical sense, when serving, you are putting yourself out there in front of the church's leadership. The leaders of the church will realize your servant's heart and may give you more responsibility as time progresses. You could be leading whatever service team you were once a newbie on in no time. Leadership opportunities are abundant when Jesus is at the heart of what you are doing.

Ultimately, serving in the church allows you to actively live out the teachings of Jesus Christ, becoming a living testimony of his love and grace to others. Volunteer in church and see where it takes you. Maybe you get to use some God-given talents to better the world. Perhaps you figure out what your skills are by selflessly volunteering in church. The important thing is that you give it a shot. Even if it is saying hello to someone and handing them a church bulletin, volunteering in the house of God is essential. Every job matters because it focuses on bringing others to the point where they are ready to give their life to Jesus Christ and be saved. Without every church volunteer, keeping people and baptizing them in the name of the Father, Son, and Holy Ghost could not have happened. Every believer is essential and has a place to serve within the church. Give it a shot. You will be happy you did!

Keep It Simple Step: Volunteer at your church or a local shelter, participate in community service projects, or help a needy neighbor. Jesus taught the importance of serving others selflessly. A quick internet search will give you many serving opportunities in your area. My personal favorite is Habitat for Humanity. It's a good cause and teaches me how to do common household repairs.

Whoever is generous to the poor lends to the Lord, and he will repay him for his deed.

—Proverbs 19:17

Fresh out of the Baptismal Pool

Read and journal on 1 Corinthians 12:13.

CHAPTER 8
LEADERSHIP

When he had finished washing their feet, he put on his clothes and returned to his place. "Do you understand what I have done for you?" he asked them. "You call me 'Teacher' and 'Lord,' and rightly so, for that is what I am. Now that I, your Lord and Teacher, have washed your feet, you also should wash one another's feet. I have set you an example that you should do as I have done for you. Very truly, I tell you, no servant is greater than his master, nor is a messenger greater than the one who sent him. Now that you know these things, you will be blessed if you do them.

—John 13:12–17

When you think about leaders, who comes to mind? When I think about this question, my mind wanders to figures like the president, generals, CEOs, and quarterbacks—polished men and women who command respect and exercise authority over regular folks like me. But biblically and historically speaking, what kind of people did God call to lead and use to expand his kingdom here on Earth? The most straightforward answer is those willing to answer the celestial phone when called. He did not look at statistics like credentials or education like human resources people would when applying for a job. He did not search for the strongest, most put-together, attractive person. God saw heart! God chose leaders by looking at them from the inside and equipping them to do his work. Even if you have never thought of yourself as a leader or allowed to lead, please understand that once you become a Christian, you are a leader. Jesus Christ is the church's leader, and when you became saved, you asked him to come into your heart. The Holy Spirit entered your body at that moment, and you became a new person. A newborn leader and soldier for Christ!

The best leaders, traditionally, are excellent followers. In the previous chapter, I discussed the importance of serving and volunteering. By making yourself available to serve, you opened pathways to advance in leadership throughout the church. You build on those experiences of serving to benefit when your ticket is called to lead. If you currently do not see yourself in a leadership role, wait. The only constant in life is change. Someone on your service team will have a life-altering event; before you know it, you are the head of the hospitality team or something similar. But do not be scared. You came into the role with an open heart, and God will reward you by equipping you.

It is all part of the process. For over two thousand years, the business of changing the world and carrying the gospel has been handed off to subsequent generations. Plus, the Great Commission forces us to become leaders by going out into the world and making more disciples. Embrace it! The Savior of the world calls you to lead others to Christ, to lead others to salvation from the torments of sin, Hell, and the grave. When you become a follower of Christ, you become a leader.

But what if you are nervous about leading? What if you do not feel ready or able? If you read this book, I understand you are probably still wet from the baptismal pool. If you google "how many books on leadership are there," you will find that, as of today, there are over 56,136 books written on leadership. That number alone overwhelms me. All those books are probably good and based on tons of research and life experiences at different levels of leadership in various industries, etc. I will argue that all those 56,000+ books are foundationally based on the Bible. The Bible holds several lessons and teachings on leadership. It also flips the narrative of what we think leadership looks like.

Most of us grew up with or remember seeing the food pyramid with the pointy peak at the top. Lots of us feel like that is how leadership works. Your big boss is at the tip-top, and more and more people expand the base the further down you look. We tend to see it in a socioeconomic sense. The person at the top holds all the power and is better than the rest of us. That we, at the bottom, work to make him more robust and better. As my father would so eloquently put it, stuff rolls downhill. The Bible teaches us that the opposite is true about leadership. That the pyramid shape needs to be flipped upside down. The prominent boss leader at the tip-top is supposed to hold up the rest of the pyramid. This is called servant leadership. It is what is taught in the Bible and what all 56,000+ books are trying to explain.

What does this mean for you, a brand-new follower of Christ? It means that the more you put yourself in positions of service for the church, the more you will develop and be seen as a leader. I know it contradicts what we have all been taught, right? A few chapters back, I mentioned that things in this world are not always seen the same in the eyes of Christ. Several passages in the Bible support this. For example, "The meek will inherit the Earth." That makes no sense in today's modern world. It goes against everything we have been taught. So, yes, a brand-new Christ follower who helps every third Sunday of the month in the parking lot ministry has the propensity to be a church leader. It just takes time and an openness to Jesus.

So, how do you ensure you are the best leader that you can be for Jesus Christ? Well, you can use this book as a guide in that endeavor. Several factors are going to form you as a Christian leader. They range from developing a solid spiritual foundation rooted in the Bible to guiding other people in discerning the plans of God. Please understand that this will not happen overnight. This consists of a lifetime of consistent growth that will allow you to become a leader for Jesus. Let us practically break down the steps required to rise through the ranks and become a general in the Lord's army.

> <u>Halftime Scripture</u>: *Be strong and very courageous. Be careful to obey all the law my servant Moses gave you; do not turn from it to the right or the left, that you may be successful wherever you go. Keep this Book of the Law always on your lips; meditate on it day and night so that you may be careful to do everything written in it. Then you will be prosperous. Have I not commanded you? Be strong and courageous. Do not be afraid; do not be discouraged, for the Lord your God will be with you wherever you go.*
>
> —*Joshua 1:7–9*

The first step in ensuring you become a strong Christian leader is to solidify yourself firmly in the Word of God. Since you have accepted Christ as your savior, you already have a solid relationship with him. He lives inside your heart. Now, it is up to you to decipher the Word of God and then put it into practice. Live within the pages of the Bible. Soak up all the knowledge it has written on the pages. Become smart in all things Bible!

Next, operate with total honesty and integrity. You are probably wondering what exactly that means. It means getting right with everything in your life. Repent and turn away from all the sins you have been hiding in secret. Down to the most minor fib on your resume! If you are battling a sin requiring professional help, seek assistance. Many churches have free or low-cost counseling services to help you improve your life. Change it all to reflect who you are as a genuine person. God cannot do anything with a fake version of yourself, but he can build civilizations on the shoulders of a natural and authentic person. Develop your character in a Christ-like manner. Get honest with the person in the mirror. Repent and reap the benefits of humbling yourself before God.

Additionally, look for opportunities to educate yourself in a Christ-like manner. Take classes in biblical studies. Many churches have partnered with Bible colleges in the area and have self-paced correspondence courses that you can take. Often, these are free or low-cost. If you desire to, you can advance your education into a theological realm of study and earn actual degrees and certificates. Ask your pastors about any leadership training programs, like internships, available at the church. Most churches have internship programs. They are usually about a year long, and you can learn about all the ministries your church participates in. It is an eye-opening experience to see how much work is involved both within and outside the church's walls. Should you feel called to go this route, seek advice from pastors and staff in effective communication. For example, take an evangelism class. Many churches offer evangelism classes that teach regular people to proclaim the gospel publicly. If your church does not provide a class like that, sign up for a public speaking class at a local community college. Educate yourself both formally and informally in all things Jesus Christ.

Central to Christian leadership is personal spiritual growth. This includes things like regular prayer, consistent church attendance, and fasting. You must learn to rely on prayer for guidance. You must develop a relationship with your local church. You must practice art forms like fasting that align you with God's plan for your life. Developing a consistent habit of these methods of spiritual growth helps leaders make decisions in step with biblical principles and God's plan. Develop a plan for prayer in your life. Go to church consistently. Humble yourself before God by fasting. The strongest leaders are those kneeling before God in every decision they must make.

The most significant growth in your leadership will happen through your ability to reach out and serve others. This is where you will cut your teeth, refine your leadership style, and hone your leadership skills. By serving others, you will understand the nuances of servant leadership. You will collaborate and network with great people who foster a heart for the Lord's work. Reach out to your pastor and build your leadership repertoire by serving in some capacity in the church. Every little bit counts. God can use the smallest of actions by you and multiply them beyond your wildest dreams. So, look for volunteer or serving opportunities and lead by putting others first.

This final step contradicts our American ideals and goes against everything we are taught growing up. To develop as a leader for Christ, you must surrender to his purpose in your life. Ephesians 2:10 explains this brilliantly. It says, "For we are God's handiwork, created in Christ Jesus to do good works, which God prepared in advance for us to do." We must search ourselves and our gifts to see what Jesus wants us to do. Find our purpose in him. I am not saying vocational ministry, or ministry where you work, is not viable. I am simply saying that your purpose in life is not to make a bunch of shareholders in a boardroom somewhere a lot of money. Your career is a tool. It is not your identity. When you accept

Jesus Christ, your identity now lies in him. Figure out your spiritual gift and his purpose for your life. Surrender yourself to it, and then watch how Christ uses your God-given talents to lead others to Jesus Christ.

Every leader needs to understand what their mission is. Regardless of your socioeconomic standing, you have one mission after you pop out of the water soaking wet on a Sunday. That is to show and tell everyone you encounter about Jesus Christ. You lead others to a new life in Christ by planting that seed of faith. The president of the USA, a corporate CEO, a military general, and a football quarterback can lead millions of men and women in a lifetime. However, that fact does not matter if those important people do not lead those millions of followers to Jesus Christ. It matters infinitely more if you lead just one person to Jesus Christ. Entrust yourself to the biblical leadership development process with Jesus Christ. Keep him at the center of everything you do, and you will lead others to the actual Promised Land with Jesus Christ.

Keep It Simple Step: Maintain a positive outlook even in challenging circumstances, trusting God's plan and provision. Let your life reflect the hope and joy of a relationship with Jesus. With anything complex, remember that you *get to* do something, not *have to* do something. Those two little words are a game-changer. Plus, positivity breeds positivity. Even the negative Nancy in your group will work harder, so you quit being so positive.

> *Where there is no guidance, people fall, but in an abundance of counselors, there is safety.*
>
> *—Proverbs 11:14*

Read and journal on Galatians 3:27.

CHAPTER 9
EVANGELISM

Go therefore and make disciples of all the nations, baptizing them in the name of the Father, the Son, and the Holy Spirit, teaching them to observe all things that I have commanded you; and lo, I am with you always, even to the end of the age.

—*Matthew 28: 19–20*

More people are afraid to speak publicly than are afraid to die. Just think about that for a second. When asked if someone would rather give a speech in front of some people or die, they chose death! What does that say about public speaking? Public speaking is frightening for a lot of people, and I am sure that when you saw the title "Evangelism" in a book about steps in growing with God after being saved, you might have had a mixed reaction. I almost did not add this chapter to the book, but it is vitally important. In its simplest form, evangelism is speaking the gospel of Christ through public and personal testimony. Yes, evangelism is spoken in front of packed churches and football stadiums, but it is also done in smaller groups and one-on-one conversations with people. The greatest gift anyone can ever receive is the gift of salvation through Christ Jesus. Why wouldn't you want to extend that gift to everyone you know?

But I know you are reading this and thinking you are not Billy Graham. You have never set foot in a Bible college. You may be an introvert. You might have had a horrible high school performance of *Oklahoma*; you froze on stage and forgot all your lines. Maybe you discovered Christ, and a friend handed you this book. How is a novice follower of Christ supposed to spread the gospel and practice evangelism? These are all significant concerns. Do not let this overwhelm you. Let's start small.

The first step in being an excellent evangelist is loving Jesus. You cannot spread the gospel of Christ if you do not believe it with all your heart. People will be encouraged by Satan to pick apart their faith publicly. Remember, Satan cannot get you anymore, but he can minimize your impact on the world by casting doubt in those you are trying to spread the gospel to. This foundational love for Jesus will give you the strength to battle hecklers and naysayers because you know deep down what Christ has saved you from. But remember that every foundation is set upon footers. Your foundational love of Christ needs to be built upon the footers of the wisdom of the Bible. Through the Word of God comes wisdom and love for Jesus. Build your love of Jesus from the pages of this excellent book. Plus, the more knowledgeable you are in Christ, the more credibility you will carry into the mission field.

Own your testimony. Some of you might wonder what that means, which is okay. Your testimony is your personal story of how you came to be saved by Jesus. No two testimonies are ever the same because we are all unique people. Some people become saved early in life, others later. Christ saves some through harrowing ordeals. Some people have family members who introduce them to Christ. Some people feel something when they accept Christ. Some do not. No matter what, your testimony matters in the field of evangelism. It is your personal story of how you came to know and love Jesus. Do not be embarrassed by it. Capitalize on it. If you have a substance use disorder of some kind, own it. A criminal, own it. An average guy just walking down the street going through the motions of life, own it. Your unique testimony has the potential to reach someone going through the same thing you went through. By owning your testimony and speaking boldly about how Jesus changed your life, you can impact others for the glory of God. Simply put, be yourself and tell your story of redemption. No matter how awful, boring, or whatever adjective you insert in the subject line, your story matters and can change someone else's life!

Public speaking is terrifying, and I get that. But knowing that neighbors and loved ones will spend an eternity in Hell should scare you more. You probably do not think you have an adequate platform to spread the gospel, but you do. A common theme in this book is to start small. So, the next step in spreading the gospel is something that you probably already do. The next time you go to a restaurant to eat out, say a prayer before eating. It is a public declaration of thanksgiving and love for Christ in the safety of your friends and family. It is the perfect place to start to evangelize. By praying "in Jesus's name," you invite the Holy Spirit to surround you and invade the restaurant or whatever establishment you are in. Plus, it is an attention-getter. Countless times, after I have prayed before a meal, strangers come up to me and say how refreshing it is to see a family pray together. It opens a comfortable and supportive dialogue. Most importantly, it plants seeds of Christ into the other people's minds at the restaurant because they see and maybe hear you pray before a meal. It is the perfect starting point for spreading the gospel. Build on your evangelistic confidence through small public prayers!

Another way to take a small step in evangelism is to answer people's questions truthfully and without a politically correct filter. Everyone around you will notice how you have "changed" since you became a follower of Jesus, and rightly so. You have changed! You have been born again. But more than likely, Dave in accounting was not at your baptism on Sunday, so he will not understand why you are different. People whom you encounter every day may ask questions. Be ready to answer them humbly and respectfully. Do not start shoving Jesus down everyone's throats; that will only deter people. Instead, answer their questions truthfully and away from the crowds at the watercooler. People are more willing to be honest about their faith in private. Use these private conversations to work on your evangelical message. You never know; Dave from accounting might be in the pew next to you on Sunday, and it was all due to your respectful evangelical conversation at the watercooler.

Vulnerability is terrifying. I understand that our society teaches us to be stoic. However, to grow, you must learn to be confident, vulnerable, and comfortable sharing your testimony in front of different people. Your testimony may not be pretty. You may think that it might make people uncomfortable because your previous life before Christ was filled with sin. You may feel embarrassed or ashamed of your earlier life before Jesus. So, how do you overcome this and become comfortable showing the world the skeletons in your closet? Depending on what the sin is, professional therapy may be an excellent place to start. However, as a church, we are supposed to bear one another's burdens. A few chapters ago, I discussed the benefits of being in a small group during the week. Your small group is the perfect place to be vocally vulnerable in a safe and loving environment. Talking about your sin and how you have changed your life since accepting Jesus with your small group, you practice confident vulnerability in a public setting. Do not be ashamed of your past. The bigger the disaster, the more amazing God is in the restoration. Share this truth with loved ones in your small group and reap the evangelical growth.

> <u>Halftime Scripture:</u> *How beautiful on the mountains are the feet of those who bring good news, who proclaim peace, who bring good tidings, who proclaim salvation, who say to Zion, "Your God reigns!"*
>
> —*Isaiah 52:7*

Now understand that throughout your talks with people about Christ, people will have questions that you cannot answer. Deep questions. Sometimes, you may feel like Dave from the accounting department minored in ancient Western civilization. Do not be discouraged.

If you do not know the answer to his question, write it down and then research the topic. Then, revisit the conversation. In doing this, you are doing multiple things. The first is that you are making yourself smarter as a Christ follower. Next, you show whoever had the question that they mattered. The fact that you spent time researching a topic or question they had should show them how important Christ is to you. Finally, it shows the credibility that you now have as a believer and evangelist. Admitting that you did not know something, then proceeding to research it, then explaining it to that person proves your integrity to Christ. This is called apologetics. Apologetics is a defense of the Christian faith. If you go on Amazon right now, you will be overwhelmed by the many books about apologetics. Pick one up and read it. Learn how to hone your skills in defending your faith and walk with Christ. This will only help you in spreading the good news about Jesus!

Occasionally, your church may do a mission trip. A mission trip is when church members travel outside the community to spread the gospel. Traditionally, this involves some form of outreach project, like assisting in building a well or school. It is improving an impoverished community in the name of Jesus. This sounds like a perfect place to practice evangelically. In going on a mission, you are doing exactly what Christ commanded. You are going out into the world and showing everyone your love of Jesus by helping others outside your community. Your message does not have to be perfect. There may be a language barrier. But the evangelical action in joyfully working on behalf of Christ for others speaks volumes. Utilize this time on a mission to gain valuable knowledge in love. See the power of Christ in sacrificial giving. Look at how less fortunate people can find joy in Christ amidst hardships you have never imagined. Take a mental picture of what the church is supposed to look like in its simplest form. Talk to people you have nothing in common with except a love for Jesus. Gain an education in humility and blessings. Then, turn around and use what you have been a part of in the mission field to talk about it to people. By going on a mission trip, you now have experience being the literal hands and feet of the church. You can draw from your experiences in the field to further your evangelical prowess.

I know you are wondering when I would talk about the greatest evangelist the world has ever known, Billy Graham. Simply put, that man had a gift. He was a powerful speaker and could back it up with living an excellent, Christ-centered life. But you and I are not Billy Graham. God utilized his gifts and talents for the kingdom and will use your gifts and talents, too. How will he do it? I cannot say. Evangelism takes so many forms. Remember, it is the public spreading of the gospel. There are many ways to do this.

One of my favorite forms of evangelism is the big sign bullhorn guys usually find outside significant events saying, "Jesus is Coming Back!" or "Repent the End is Near." I'm not being sarcastic here. I am always amazed at how brave those people are. Just think about how ridiculed they must be by people who pass by. They are courageous people and must have deep convictions to go before strangers to football games or concerts and tell the truth. Because, if you follow Christ, you know that Jesus is coming back! That the end is near! Maybe not in an Armageddon sense yet, but it seems like everyone gets around seventy-five to ninety-five years before they get to meet Jesus. However, even in an Armageddon sense, Christ is returning. He promised he would, and everyone needs to know the truth.

If that is not your cup of tea, you can always utilize social media to spread the gospel. Social media is a great way to reach millions of people. As we discussed earlier, start small. Maybe share a Billy Graham revival message on Facebook. Post a Bible verse from which you drew inspiration. These little things add up. You never know which friend will see your post or video and have a life-changing seed planted in them by something you posted. The Holy Spirit is everywhere. The Holy Spirit is the original Wi-Fi network of the world, and it is guaranteed to have the fastest and most reliable speed.

You may be called to be an evangelist. Ephesians 4:11 talks about the different gifts God gives to the people. Perhaps you work in a vocational role where you speak publicly often. It does not frighten you to get up in front of people and give presentations. You may have to provide weekly sales pitches for your company to new clients. The gift of evangelism may already be within you. If this is the case, consider yourself lucky because you are already ahead of everyone else. Use this gift for the good of God. Instead of selling material products and services, sell your life-giving testimony of how Jesus saved you. Look at your spiritual gift and proclaim Jesus.

I have spoken mostly about more minor ways to impact the world evangelically. To gain confidence in preaching the gospel to people. Over time and with practice, you will become more comfortable preaching, and the audience size will grow. Remember to be consistent in studying the Word of God. Depending on the path and doors and windows God opens for you, it may behoove you to investigate advanced degrees of education. I do not know your current education level, and the Bible does not say an advanced degree in theology is necessary, but it would not hurt. Biblically-based education programs arguably deal with the most important thing a person can study: salvation. Lots of colleges offer degrees in religious and biblical studies. Ask your pastor where he received his degree from and investigate it. Most Christian colleges are online and have flexible classes. Advancing your education will only help you to go out and bring the gospel to the world.

Evangelism is scary. Public speaking is scary. Traveling to third-world countries is worrisome. Going against the grain at work, school, and heaven forbid, social media is frightening! I understand that. But we are all called to spread the gospel to the corners of the Earth. We must be brave. We must be educated. We must trust in Jesus. We must allow ourselves to be his conduit in proclaiming his message to the world. Even though you may be young in the faith, understand that you may be called to give your testimony one day in front of others. Do not fail others by not being ready to proclaim the name of Jesus. Start small. Be humble. Speak boldly in love about the one true King of the world!

Keep It Simple Step: Be willing to share your testimony and beliefs with others when opportunities arise. Respectfully discuss your faith journey and how Jesus has impacted your life. Since you are probably not Billy Graham, here is a simple way to reach out and evangelize your world. At the end of every email or letter, I write "In Christ" before I sign my name. That simple sign-off brings Christ to every person, even for a split second.

The fruit of the righteous is a tree of life, and whoever captures souls is wise.

—Proverbs 11:30

Read and journal on Ephesians 4:4–6.

CHAPTER 10
REFLECTION AND PRAYER

Answer me when I call to you, my righteous God. Give me relief from my distress; have mercy on me and hear my prayer.

—Psalms 4:1.

I saved the most important thing—to help a new Christ follower out—for last. Prayer is huge. The importance of prayer cannot be understated. It is your personal phone line to God. It is your celestial call line to the heavens. Understanding who, what, where, when, why, and how to pray is essential. The easy answer to all those questions is you, everything, anywhere, anytime, for anything, and in every position imaginable. I will discuss some of the nuances in this chapter. Prayer is something that I am still working on mastering. Amazingly, the creator of the universe cares about how I am doing! This is so contrary to our current culture. Where most people are self-obsessed or do not even realize they exist. That is what is so incredible about our God. He sees you, hears you, and wants you. Prayer is the way to the Father's always listening ear. Reflection is just as critical because it lets you see how God moved in your life. It shows how God answered your prayer or why he didn't. Prayer and reflection are the start and finish of things that are important to you. Please note that God is not your genie, and not all prayers are answered the way you want them to be answered. There is a bigger plan at play than the one inside your head.

If you google "how to pray according to the Bible," you will be confused. Some recommendations have three steps, some five, and some say to call out to God like a friend. Is there a correct way to pray? A proper position or time of day? I am not intelligent by any stretch of the imagination, but I know that the answer comes from the Bible. Since the Bible is about Jesus, I should look at how he prayed. Matthew 6: 9–13 and Luke 11:2–4 discuss how Jesus told his disciples to pray. This prayer is called the "Lord's Prayer," which is an excellent place to start. Matthew 6:9–13 is the more extended version of the prayer. The one found in Luke is a shortened version. You have probably prayed it many times. It goes:

Our Father in Heaven, Hallowed be Your name. Your kingdom comes. Your will be done on Earth as it is in Heaven. Give us this day our daily bread. And forgive us our debts as we forgive our debtors. And do not lead us into temptation but deliver us from the evil one. For Yours is the kingdom and the power and the glory forever. Amen.

This prayer is precisely what Jesus told us to pray in the Bible, and I think it covers all the topics a human being can come up against. It is the prayer coming from the only perfect person, Jesus Christ.

But digging deeper into the Bible, I found that Jesus prayed to God in various ways. It does not seem like there was a standard operating procedure for prayer. He called out to his Father at all times of day, in different positions, and in all other types of emotional states of mind. I can deduce from his prayers that they came from the heart and that he loved and respected his Father, God!

I feel like that is an excellent place to start, by having reverence for the Almighty God. Just like I talked about respecting the Holy Bible, show respect to God during prayer. You would not just storm into your boss's office at work, kick up your feet on his desk, call him by his first name, and then make a list of demands. And he is just your boss! So don't think about coming at God like that. He is the creator of the world and sent his one and only Son to die so that you may live, so I feel like he deserves some respect with a capital R. There is no need to get fancy with the names or add a bunch of adjectives before and after his name. God knows who he is. The Bible says that the demons flee from hearing the name of Jesus. Call out to your Father in Heaven. He is awaiting your call! Just remember who he is and that he oversees everything.

Next, clear the air with the Lord. What I mean by that is to ask forgiveness for the things that you have done wrong. God knows what you did, but by acting and bringing your sins before him, you recognize that he is the only one who can fix your problems. This is the first step in the church's art form of repentance. Admit to him that you scr*wed up somewhere with something. You know what you did.

The next part of repentance is the hardest. That is the action of turning away entirely from sin. But that is a subject for another book. So, admit your wrongdoings to the Lord. Like most fathers, he is understanding and has already forgiven you. That is what is so unbelievable to me. Once you accepted Christ into your heart, you were forgiven and made new in the Lord. Jesus died for your past, present, and future sins. Is grace not mind-blowing? Gain a clean slate and conscience with the Lord before you make your request.

Remember that nothing is off-limits to God because He is omnipotent. He already knows and understands your struggles. Suppose you ate that unmarked yogurt in the office break room. Confess it! If you broke a vase at your grandma's house. Confess it! If you dinged someone's car in the parking lot and forgot to leave a note, some things are unforgivable, but... Just kidding! Confess that, too! Confess your sins to him! The Bible says in 1 John 1:9: "If we confess our sins, he is faithful and just to forgive us our sins and to cleanse us from all unrighteousness." Understand that God does not like your sin, but he was willing to send his Son on the cross to die for you, so he wants to forgive you.

Once you have done those two things, pour your heart out to the Lord. He hears you. He knows what you are going through and is ready to help you. Just realize that it will not be on your timetable or happen precisely how you would like. He is in charge. He works miracles in the background that you cannot even dream of. We think we know the master plan, but we have no idea. So, pour your heart into him and let him get to work. It does not matter how big or little your issue or prayer request is. He wants to hear it all. Ensure you send up some celestial thank you notes and your prayer requests. Even amid the struggle, we are so blessed. Make sure to give praise to the Lord. Whatever is in your heart, pour it out to him completely. Do not hold anything back. Give it all to the Lord!

Do not be afraid to pray for other people, either. God wants you to do that. Praying for others during your prayer time shows spiritual growth and maturity. Pray for our world leaders, for people you know who are sick, for those who are less fortunate in the world than us, for your church, and for your community. You do not need to know the person personally to pray for them.

> <u>Halftime Scripture:</u> *If my people, who are called by my name, will humble themselves and pray and seek my face and turn from their wicked ways, then I will hear from heaven, and I will forgive their sin and heal their land.*
>
> *—2 Chronicles 7:14*

When I first started attending a Bible study, the leader would take prayer requests. I remember people in the Bible study requesting prayers for people they hardly even knew, like my sister's cousin's uncle from a different momma kind of situation prayer requests. I thought that was strange when I first started attending. However, I realized those people were more spiritually mature than me. They had learned that prayer is not a selfish thing. It is a God thing, and God covers the world. By considering themselves with others, they were doing an intercessory prayer. It is incredible to think that someone or a group of people may be praying for you right now. Isn't our God a fantastic God? Aren't you excited and happy that you took the plunge and became a part of the church of Jesus Christ?

Finally, give thanks to the Lord when you close your prayer. A few paragraphs earlier, I talked about reverence for the Lord. Show him some respect when you wrap up your prayer. A "thank you" can go a long way. Plus, we should thank the world's creator for listening to us. We do not deserve any of this. The Bible makes it clear that we deserve death. However, God so loved us that he gave his only begotten Son so that whoever believes shall have eternal life (John 3:16). Give thanks to the Lord for listening, caring, and eventually fixing our problems. Then slap a hearty "amen" at the end of the prayer. Amen means "so be it," which is a great way to end a heartfelt message on a two-way radio to the Lord. It's an old-school way of saying "over and out." Bring all your issues, good and bad, to God and let him work. It will truly blow you away when you see what he did in your life.

Which leads me to reflection. When I was going through my divorce, I was trying to understand the hurt, pain, suffering, and a slew of other feelings that I was having. I would wake up around five in the morning before the kids were up, pray, and cry into a cup of black coffee. One day, I picked up an old spiral notebook, and for some reason, started writing my prayers to God. I don't know why I did it, but I did. Every day for about forty-six days, I wrote the most gut-wrenching prayers to God, asking for him to show up and heal my marriage. Fix me, fix her, fix us so that she would return and we could be a family again. I would ask God to care for us financially because it was tight. Protect the kids and keep everyone healthy. I logged my prayers. I mostly forgot about my notebook until about a year later.

I remember looking for a password I had written down for a website. I stumbled across the prayers and read them. I remembered the anguish that I'd felt on those many early mornings. However, I gained a sense of strength that the Lord God Almighty did not leave me in that pit. No! He was with me in the pit and had me climb out of it. I was still grieving in some ways from my divorce, but I saw how far I had come from those mornings in December of 2020 and January and February of 2021. I was able to reflect on my life and how much God was with me in the suck and muck of it all. That is what reflection does.

Reflection is precisely seeing who, what, where, when, why, and how God worked in your life. Reflection shows you how God answered your prayers. It was not in my time, but I saw how God used his time to work in my life. It was amazing when I took time out of my busy schedule to see God's handiwork on my life. The hardest thing to find today is spare time. I completely understand that. However, to fully grasp the goodness of God, you must unplug from the world for a minute and breathe. Carve out at least a few moments to meditate and see the amazing things God has walked with you through.

What are some tips on reflection? I only have a few that I can think of. My memory is horrible, so I write down important things. The first would be to start a prayer journal. You can keep it in a notebook or type it on a Word document. Whatever you would like to do. Since you are new to the faith, starting a prayer journal provides a record of God's faithfulness so that you can see how Christ shaped your life as a new Christian. Put the date at the top of the page and write your prayer. Add a Bible verse or a memory that is also important to you about that day. Documentation of what was on your mind at that moment in history is neat to look back on years later. It will show how far you have come in your journey with Christ.

Next, unplug the electronics and television and escape the doldrums of society for a little while. Turn off the phone and leave it somewhere while you meditate on the word and clear your heart and mind to receive God's influence on your life. The Bible says in 1 Kings 19:12–13, "After the earthquake a fire, but the LORD was not in the fire: and after the fire a still small voice. And it was so, when Elijah heard it, that he wrapped his face in his mantle, went out, and stood in the cave entrance." God was in a still, small voice. Not the pundits on CNN or Fox News. Not the Facebook post of your friend Becky bragging about the cruise she went on. Not the TikTok video about the dance that all the people are doing. God is in the quiet. Not the noise. Remember, God is not going to play second fiddle in anything. He is front and center. He wants you to have reverence for him and put him before everything else. That is why he speaks in a still, small voice. He wants to ensure that you are focused on him and listening because what he has to say is the most important thing ever. Get rid of all the distractions. I know it is hard to do, but remember that twenty years ago, we did not have these distractions, and life was exemplary without them. Turn off the phones and pick up the celestial prayer line. The creator of the universe wants to talk to you. By cutting out distractions, you will feel empowered and in control of your spiritual journey.

Another tip for reflection is to have a serene, quiet place to empty your mind and focus on God. For many of us, including myself, anxiety tends to disrupt this time. My head plays tricks on me whenever I am in a quiet place. I begin thinking about everything I need to do, how I will do it, etcetera. None of that stuff matters. What matters is Jesus. With practice, you can learn to meditate and relax your mind enough to see how God is working in your life. I recommend an area away from the stressors of life. If you ever wonder why your dad, brother, or husband stays in the bathroom for forty-five minutes a day, it is probably because that is where he can clear his head and no one will bother him. In all seriousness, find a place to clear your head after prayer and quiet your mind briefly. Cut out the malarkey and focus on God.

Focus on breathing. Yes, breathing. Once you successfully quiet your mind and body, breathe. Take the stress out of your life. Stress is a distraction from Jesus. Just focus on breathing, and let Jesus show you how he has worked in your life recently. We are a society bombarded with tasks and stuff that do not matter. By clearing our heads and relaxing our bodies, we allow Jesus to strengthen our souls.

If you have doubts about the importance of prayer and reflection, I will point you to a document showing its validity. If you look at the Bible and Psalms, notice what happens when you read them. Psalms is a collection of poems, songs, and prayers written over a thousand years. These psalms are very similar to a prayer journal. Seeing how God worked in people's lives thousands of years ago and continues to work in people now is fantastic. If it was good enough for King David, King Solomon, and all the other kings of Israel to do, I think it would also benefit your life.

Prayer and reflection both take practice. Pray and reflect as often as you can. God is listening and wants you to reach out and give all your struggles to him.

Usually, we go to prayer as a final resort, but it needs to be the very first thing we do. God wants us to put him front and center in our lives. The best thing you can do is always pray to him! Then, when you finally get a moment to reflect, you will see the mountains that God moved to get you exactly where he knew you belonged. Pray constantly and about everything.

Keep It Simple Step: Forgive those who have wronged you, just as Jesus forgave us. Letting go of grudges and showing grace can be a powerful testament to one's faith. Please write a letter forgiving someone who wronged you, buy a stamp, and send it. Do not be surprised by the power of forgiveness when that person reaches out and wants to rekindle a friendship.

> *The Lord is far from the wicked, but he hears the prayer of the righteous.*
>
> *—Proverbs 15:29*

Fresh out of the Baptismal Pool

Read and journal on Colossians 2:9–13.

CONCLUSION

Therefore, my beloved brethren, be steadfast, immovable, always abounding in the work of the Lord, knowing that your labor is not in vain in the Lord.

—*1 Corinthians 15:58*

You made it to the end of the book. Congratulations. Now on to the test that begins on the next page. Haha, that made you turn the page. Don't worry; there is no test. We live in victory every day because Christ died for our sins. However, in following Christ, the world and Satan are going to hate us and throw everything at their disposal to try to minimize your impact on the kingdom. Continue to fight on! Look around; the world does not need any more weak and run-down individuals. The world needs Jesus, and the only way the world gets more of Jesus is through your heroism in taking up your cross and following his teachings.

I understand it isn't easy. As mentioned in the earlier chapters, I struggled mightily in my walk with Christ. I did not ask many questions, take suggestions, and follow guidance from more seasoned Christ followers. Do not be me! Use the roadmap and tips in this book and train yourself like a soldier in the army of Christ. The enemy will throw hardships and troubles your way. Fight the good fight by leaning into the actual church body of believers. It seems contrarian, but being vulnerable and open is how Christ builds you up and strengthens you.

I understand that we went over a lot in the book. I know I was very detailed on how to go about doing things. I was so thorough because no one told me what the next steps should be. I want you to succeed and bring glory to God as efficiently as possible. It may look overwhelming, but when all is said and done, there are just ten things a new believer needs to do after being saved by Christ:

1. Join a local church.
2. Understand that the devil is accurate and that he is going to try to exploit your sins to stop you

from making an impact on this world for Jesus Christ.
3. Treat the church sermon like a college lecture and attend regularly.
4. Come up with a Bible reading plan and READ your Bible.
5. Join a small group or Bible study outside the church walls.
6. Find a Christian mentor and become a disciple.
7. Volunteer as part of a service team at church as your schedule allows.
8. Be open to leadership opportunities in the church.
9. Share your testimony and the gospel with everyone you meet.
10. Build up your prayer life. Talk to God constantly and notice how he is working in your life.

When you get down to the nitty-gritty of everything, what to do after being saved and baptized is simple. It is all about growing and letting the family of God nurture you. It is just like growing up in a regular public school. Think of it like this: The school administration and other students are the church. The church building is a school where you go and learn. The Bible is your textbook. Your small group is the friends you hang out with after school. Your church mentor is an incredible teacher you could talk to and seek advice from. The team you serve on at church is whatever club or sports team you played for in school. Your leadership opportunities are like those you had when you tried out for student government. Your testimony is when you talk to your friends and family about something important to you in the hallways. Your prayer life is those little prayers you prayed before a big science test. The entirety of everything we talked about is growth. But instead of growing your mind and social skills like in school, you are growing spiritually in Jesus Christ.

I would be remiss if I did not discuss the lynchpin in everything discussed in the book. Consistency is vital in your walk with Christ. Be consistent in attending church. Be consistent in attending a Bible study. Be consistent in studying the Bible. Be consistent in prayer and reflection. Be consistent in serving. Be consistent in loving God and people. How do you eat an elephant? One bite at a time. It is the same in living life as a follower of Christ. Be consistent in everything you do for Christ!

> <u>Halftime Scripture</u>: *Then I saw a new heaven and a new earth, for the first heaven and the first earth had passed away, and there was no longer any sea. I saw the Holy City, the new Jerusalem, coming down out of heaven from God, prepared as a bride beautifully dressed for her husband. And I heard a loud voice from the throne saying, "Look! God's dwelling place is now among the people, and he will dwell with them.*

They will be his people, and God will be with them and their God. He will wipe every tear from their eyes. There will be no more death or mourning or crying or pain, for the old order of things has passed away." He who was seated on the throne said, "I am making everything new!" Then he said, "Write this down, for these words are trustworthy and true."

—*Revelation 21:1–5*

How do you keep up with that consistency needed to grow? It would be best if you practiced discipline. Discipline is the catalyst of consistency. Both go hand in hand. Look at the buff folks in the gym. They did not get to be buff after a couple of intense workouts. On the contrary, they became buff by being disciplined and working out consistently over a long period. This is the same with being a follower of Christ. Consistent growth born from a disciplined routine will create an incredible soldier for the army of God.

You will fail along the way. What a positive way to wrap up a book, huh? There will be days when you do not feel like going to church. There will be days when you stay up all night with the kids, hit the snooze button, and miss your quiet time with God in the morning. There will be people in your church who you may not necessarily mesh well with. Regular life is going to happen, and Satan is going to succeed at derailing you sometimes. To take a quote from the classic movie *Gone with the Wind*, remember, "Tomorrow is another day." Make sure you give yourself the same gift your Father in Heaven gave you: the gift of grace.

Make sure that you do not get depressed when you do make a mistake. Learn to forgive yourself and give yourself a little bit of grace. Growing up was hard. Growing up again after being saved and baptized in a world that despises you is even more complicated. Just think about how many times you failed at things the first time you tried them growing up. But remember that you got the hang of it after a few tries. The same thing goes with being a Christian. No one is perfect except Jesus Christ.

When you do fail, do what is right. Rectify and apologize for whatever you did wrong and jump back onto the path, walking alongside Jesus. He probably kept talking while you were on the side of the road wallowing in your failure. He does not care that you failed at something. He cares that you get up and run back into his loving arms. God knows you messed up, and he has forgiven you. Remember that we are all like the son who took his inheritance and left his dad high and dry, like in the story of the Prodigal Son (Luke 15:11–32). Remember how that story ends. The dad runs out and hugs his son when he returns from ruining his life, throwing him a party. Understand that we are not worthy of God's love. Do yourself a favor, and don't be hard on yourself while you grow in Christ. Give yourself the same grace that God gives all his children.

I hope you enjoyed this book. I hope that it was easy to read and follow. I hope the scripture references at the beginning of each chapter opened your mind a bit. I hope the scripture selection in the middle of each chapter proclaimed a powerful message that made you want to continue reading. I hope the practical step at the end of the chapter gave you a good course of action on whatever subject I was writing about. I hope you saw the practicality of the Proverbs scripture. I hope you found inspiration in the Bible verse about water baptism before the journaling page. I hope this book was the most outstanding book you have ever read about what to do after becoming saved and baptized in the name of Jesus Christ. I hope you refer this book to others so that they can benefit from what I have learned so far walking with Christ.

Thank you so much for picking up this book and reading it. I pray that it helped you find your home and the next steps in the Christian church. Take the tips found in this book and grow in your walk with Christ. Become a strong Christian whose faith is built on the foundation of scripture, love for Jesus, and love for your fellow man. Cheers to you for becoming a follower of Christ! Now go out into the world and fulfill the great commission. I wish you nothing but the best. God bless every person who reads this book.

Keep It Simple Step: Give yourself plenty of grace in your new walk with Jesus Christ. Contrary to popular belief, no one is perfect. Do not beat yourself up if you fail or feel like you come up short in any way. The God of the universe loves you and has already forgiven you. It is okay to forgive yourself.

The Lord's curse is on the house of the wicked, but he blesses the dwelling of the righteous.

—Proverbs 3:33

Fresh out of the Baptismal Pool

Read and journal on 1 Peter 3:18–22.

ABOUT THE AUTHOR

Brandon Dusanic is, first and foremost, a devoted follower of Jesus Christ. He graduated from Trinity Baptist College in Jacksonville, Florida, and is a member of Trinity at Oakleaf in Orange Park, Florida. He is a full-time single dad to his two children, Liam and Kellyn, and his furry child, Lucy, the "Wonder Dog."

Professionally, he is a retired US navy avionics technician who spent most of his career working on helicopters in Mayport, Florida. Since his retirement, he has become an educator and entrepreneur in various roles, hoping to reach others and be an excellent example of leadership to his children and community.

For fun, Brandon enjoys traveling as often as he can. Though most of his time is spent behind a windshield chauffeuring his kids to cross-country meets and other activities, he enjoys some of the finer things that Florida living offers. He enjoys golfing, fishing, gardening, and relaxing as much as possible.

"Fortis Fortuna Adiuvat"

Made in the USA
Columbia, SC
28 October 2024